NEW
WRITING
MATTER
13

MATTER 13

Editor: Andrew Jeffrey
Deputy Editor: Oliver Hadfield

Contributing Editors:
Poetry: Oliver Hadfield, Suzanne McArdle
Script: Virginia Lowes, Vicky Morris, Mark Kirby
Short Story: Rebecca McCormick, Amanda Lomas
Novel: Anna Rogola, Andrew Jeffrey
Children's/Young Adult: Special thanks to the
following members of Sheffield Young Writers:
Martha Rhodes, Anna May Fox, Jess Wood, Betsy
Middleton, Anita Chandran and Imogen Cassels.

Designed by Eleven Design
www.elevendesign.co.uk

Published by Mews Press
Printed by Northend Creative Print Solutions

Special thanks to:
Glenn Thornley and Alys Mordecai at Eleven Design.
Professor Maurice Riordan and Professor Steven
Earnshaw at Sheffield Hallam University

ISBN 978-1-84387-369-3

www.makingwritingmatter.co.uk

MATTER showcases the best work from writers on the MA Writing at Sheffield Hallam University, alongside new poetry and prose from established writers. This year's guest contributors are poets Sean O'Brien and Alan Halsey, and novelists Simon Bestwick and Danuta Reah.

Contents

Poetry

Alan Halsey
Local Forum

Pond Street Nora could run like stink but
you'd see her sometimes
sat very still on a sack of spuds
then she'd suddenly shout
'is anyone gonna clean these fucking windows'
it was either that or
'You'll not go down Princess Street no more, fucker you'
she had a bad language problem
she reckoned they made tizer from cider and hot water
she liked to recite 'Transport coat religion' and
'you won't get me up them stairs again Charlie Cooper'
then if anyone laughed at her she'd chant
'Get thee sen a brush and gooen sweep up'
but her favourite was
'fucking well chuck 'em out of West Bar'
she meant the copshop but once
she just kept shouting
'I'll be sat ont fucking saddle'
over and over and another time
'Nar then does thar like potatoes and fish or
fish and potatoes'

Little Herbert was the man in question
Eddie Bedstead collected old wood
Rommel wore welding glasses always
Subway Cyril got the DFC
he used to wear an RAF greatcoat like Tab End Joe
and push a honda placcy everywhere he went
The Green Linnet wore heavy flour make-up
Big Ada packed a punch
she sold fruit and veg
and flowers outside the City Road Cemetery on Sundays
with a turban on her head

Nellie Wellow liked to chop
up her doors and furniture for firewood
The council would replace them
then she'd chop 'em up again
her name may have been Ivy
what an angelic voice

The Duke of Darnall
directed traffic at the end of Change Alley
in his yellow silk gloves and bowler hat
it was a shame he was called Dummy Tailor
it wasn't that he couldn't
he just didn't like talking
he used to live with Russian Edna
who was always in the Barleycorn
she got picked up in the Sportsman
found murdered in High Hazels Park
There were those who said the Duke was to blame
some old lads told me an american soldier
a lorry driver freed after 18 months
said he'd paid her 10 bob
she wasn't worth it and he asked for it back
she'd stuck it up the sleeve of her cardigan
they had a fight and this happened
not in St George's churchyard but
next to the bandstand

Bob Lockett
Henry

Henry is sitting at a dining table in the front room of a thirties semi-detached house in Sheffield. He is approximately 80 years of age and is wearing a well-worn, grey suit, tatty shirt and no tie. He is sipping tea from a chipped mug. There are family photos on the walls and mantlepiece. He glances at one particular photograph of a young woman, smiling, trying to hold her hat on in a high wind at the seaside.

Henry: *(In a northern accent)*

(Sighs)

All things must pass... so someone once said.
I miss Hope. I miss her terribly; she was my life.
We met at a fairground. I used to think that was an omen, that our lives would somehow be filled with colour, joy and fun.
As a young man, I never did understand irony.
I don't really know how I will cope without her.

(He studies his mug. It has a print of a red heart on it. Turns it in his hands.)

We courted in those days. Courted. Something the youth of today would struggle to understand. We walked out together. That wasn't a euphemism for 'shagging down an alleyway,' as I believe it is today. It was 1953 and things were decent then. We had standards.
Of course, it was frustrating... but it was right.

(Henry slurps at his tea)

We never saw each other naked in the same room with

13

the light on. Really, it's true. Never.

(Henry turns to his right as though looking out onto the landing from their bedroom)

There was a mirror, on the landing, and, if our door was slightly ajar and the bathroom door was slightly ajar (which sometimes it had to be if the bulb wasn't working properly) and you sat in exactly the right position…

(Henry has by now leaned almost right over and is pointing suggesting how much effort it took to see the mirror. He then suddenly sits upright again)

But no, never naked in the same room, with the light on. Wouldn't have been decent.

(Henry shakes his head then sips at his tea again)
(Henry addresses the audience directly)

On our wedding day I had certain expectations. I suppose we both did. It had been a lovely day. The bridesmaids looked absolutely gorgeous. Good enough to eat. Mmmnn.

(Henry drifts into the memory of the day)

The wedding night had its problems. Hope was a virtuous girl, I wouldn't have been interested in her if she wasn't. And it's a lot to ask of a girl to change in such a short time: from virginal perfection to a creature that could fulfil a grown man's desires. Perhaps that's where it all went wrong. I wasn't too demanding, of course, but she found my appetites a little challenging. Looking back now, I could have spared her some embarrassment, and perhaps a little discomfort, if I'd only been more patient. But I was young, too, and young men have fiery temperaments. That's all in the past now.

(Henry sips at his tea again, reflectively)

(His mood now lifts noticeably)

Our first holiday was Torquay. It was like a foreign land
to Hope. Most things were. We'd been married a year
and my father had already expressed concern that our
union had yet to bear fruit. I could hardly tell him the
reason. But Hope was learning to enjoy the physical side
of our relationship - slowly. She came from a farming
background where animals... *(Henry makes gestures with
his hands - lost for the right words)* just the once; it took me
a while to convince her that it doesn't always work like
that with people. Eventually, I had to promise to keep it
all simple. It took some of the sparkle out of the marriage to
be honest.

*(Henry goes to drink from his mug but then places it on the
table in front of him)*

I think it might have been the difficulty that Hope had in
getting pregnant that led to her overall chilliness in the
bedroom, and that was a difficult thing to deal with. I do
understand that failure to conceive could easily lead to
failure to enjoy and I did insist it wasn't all her fault, but
the arguments were upsetting.

*(Henry lifts his mug again and studies the picture on the side.
He then places it back on the table without drinking. His
delivery now becomes more matter-of-fact)*

My little indiscretion caused ripples in the relationship.
I would like to say I regretted it but... well, I don't. And
Hope understood. I explained to her, a man has needs
and, if his wife is unable to satisfy those needs, regardless
of reason, then that is no cause for her to blame herself.
And besides, I wasn't being unfaithful. God, no, I was
helping to save the marriage.

(Angry) Which is why I found her indiscretion so
infuriating. I mean, you don't refuse milk in your coffee
in one house and then demand cream in another, do you?'

(More matter-of-fact again)

His name was Horace. A terrible name. Hope insisted on calling him Horatio. I had to forbid that. Fortunately, when the bastard found out that Hope was a married woman, he behaved like a true gentleman and broke off the relationship immediately. It was unfortunate that I couldn't allow the situation to pass unpunished but I was fair, firm but fair. I swear, there wasn't a mark on her.

(Henry picks up his mug again)

I still keep his written apology in my wallet. I like to look at it now and again. We all need something to reaffirm our position in society sometimes. It used to make Hope very cross to see me reading it though.

(Henry takes a drink, almost empties the mug)

And that leads to the most recent unpleasantness. I was furious when I found that letter in her handbag last week. A letter from another man. I thought she had learned the first time but no, after nearly sixty years of happy, though childless, marriage, she failed, desperately.

(Henry places the mug on the table, leans back and laces his fingers across his stomach)

I realised that all my efforts had been in vain, that she had been living a lie for all those years and sharing my bed while yearning for another. "Unfulfilled," is what she said. "Unfulfilled!" My God, I gave her everything. She claimed that it was an innocent friendship, just some company to keep her sane. Well, I couldn't stand for that, could I? I had to act. And I had to act positively. I'd been too lenient before. The lesson hadn't been learned. Well, I think I got through to her this time. She certainly won't be doing any of that anymore.

(Beat)

I've put an end to it.

(Beat)

Once and for all.

(Beat)

An end...

(Blue lights flash through the window and there is a loud knocking on the door. Henry stands, picks up his coat and walks to the dining-room door. He then turns and looks back into the room. He shakes his head, turns off the light and leaves.)

Vicky Morris
When You Die

You find yourself in a waiting room. It feels strangely
familiar, like you may have been there before a long time
ago. But the you that sits there is not like the you who
would have sat in a waiting room in life. And the waiting
room is no waiting room like the ones you knew in life.

There is no clock on the wall, but you wouldn't be
interested in the time anyway because you have no
notion of time or how long you have been sat in the
waiting room. There is no secretary to ask a question, if
you'd had a question to ask. You have no concept of the
size of the room or what is beyond it. Indeed, no notion
of what is finite and what is endless. You are unable to
gather thoughts about anything.

You are aware only that you are waiting and that your
memory is suspended. Like a telephone call, you have
been put on hold. You sit in a state of calm shared by
others who are waiting. Unlike the waiting rooms in life,
no judgements are passed and no thoughts are formed.
All you know for sure is that the you that sits, is happy to
wait for as long as required.

You continually take in the nondescript room as if for the
first time. The others waiting around you do the same.
They periodically emerge or disappear through a door
with a 'Way In' or 'Way Out' sign. Who cares which? It's
all the same to you. You won't remember in the moment
following its discovery anyway.

That's about it.

No wait, I forgot in all the vagueness, the only other

WAY IN

WAY OUT

thing which might be worth noting to the living not yet dead, is that, many times you have picked up, read and been unable to process a leaflet you find on the little table attached to your chair. Its title reads 'Seven Processing Room Facts about God', in a suitable font size for your eye sight. The leaflet reads:

God has never …

- Made good use of the concepts of good and evil
- Delivered punishment or reward in or after life
- Controlled any organism or inanimate object
- Made anything with a real purpose or plan
- Needed to be worshipped
- Expected anything of you
- Been accurately conceived of

After God knows how long - and as you might have gathered from the leaflet, God doesn't know how long - you recognise a name being called as your own. You automatically stand. All at once you become acutely aware of who you were and every memory you ever had. An overwhelming tangle of sensations, notions, thoughts and experiences flow through you and out beyond the Way Out door. The only thing you process as you follow, is the contents of the public information leaflet left behind on your warm seat.

Well you did ask.

Denise Setterington
Paragliding

The pilot drifts, not upwards yet
but outwards, from the grassy bank where we stand
watching, cores in a thermal and rises,
smooth as a violin stroke, towards the sun.
Others follow, wind sings in nylon as they
graffiti the sky: primary paint splats.
None look back. That's the trick you forgot.
Or was it me, calling, 'Dad,' as you staggered
dizzy with morphine, tubes dangling like sea worms,
that made you turn? The wind caught from the wrong angle
tossed you up, then dropped you, smashing
bone till your fingers couldn't work the ropes.
The wind is from the south today, the gentlest kind.
Go to the edge. I will not call your name.

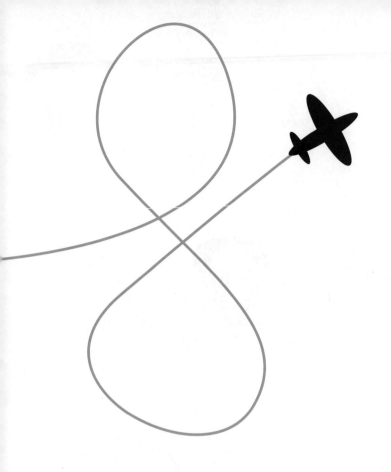

Denise Setterington
Glamour Girl

Sometimes, when the night shift are gossiping
I pull on my boots and jacket, punch in
the door code, pull both handles, one each way
and leave the ward, lay low in the sluice
count to ten then sprint down the corridor
out the fire exit, up the metal stairs

and onto the slate roof where she's waiting
darker than the July dusk. Shadows
shadow. A blade of moonlight probes
the cloud blanket as I climb her port wing
slide back her hood, drop down her cockpit door
fall into the scent of leather and Blue Grass.

Attach harness. Insert lock pin. Check:
T.M.P.F.F.R. Gyro uncaged
while the charge nurse unlocks the drugs trolley
and three televisions broadcast the news
to the soft furnishings in the day rooms.
200 yards in nine seconds, and up.

If I could find the horizon I would
hold her steady, but it doesn't matter.
We loop a figure of eight not knowing
which way's down, red lipstick, jitterbug
cloud dancing, daring the hills to rise up
rock hard, words shatter us to smithereens.

Fall. Please. Enough. Call us the glamour girls.
Big Ben's chimes interject headlines a spitfire crash,
fiscal drag, repackaged baked bean cans.
Hear the static from the wireless? *ben uncaged zo*
Blue Grass di glamour az nurse e lipstick pine
and the boy with the telegram shrugs and goes home.

Altimeter 250 feet above
the dining table. Ease the column back.
Close the throttle. Cut engines. Listen.
Whirring gyros unwinding as the pills
kick in. We were the glamour girls I've got
a photograph. See the boots, the jacket?

Linda Moss
End of the Day

Sometimes I can't face Mother. I know she's been alone all day and is waiting to hear my footsteps on the flagstones, but I need a little limbo in my own silent house before dealing with all the minor traumas that will have defined her day. I tiptoe along the path, and I've learned to unlock that formidable door in silence. I take off my shoes, sidle upstairs, avoiding the steps that creak, and hide in my study for a few minutes.

Sometimes I read. Sometimes I just stare out across the valley. The window here is so high that kites come to rest on the outside stone sill. If they notice me, they'll launch themselves downwards and fly off below my eye level, blunt bronze wings over the stream and into the pine wood. Beyond the trees the hillsides rise again steeply, tawny to dull purple and flecked with sheep.

Up here I'm a teenager again, having smuggled an illicit boyfriend into my bedroom. I don't want Mother to know that I do this.

Tonight, the moors are textured with slanting evening light, and it's possible to see the shadows of running hares. Irregular patches of snow still sculpt the higher escarpments. In the dusk, I trip over a basket of wool by the study door. I panic momentarily.

"Love?" she calls, "is that you?"

I creep downstairs. "Yes, I've just come back. I needed the loo. I'm just coming to see you."

"Oh, thank goodness you've come back. I've had such a panic."

Oh Lord, has she hurt herself again? Or just broken something? I go quickly through to her room.

"There's a cassette stuck in the recorder!" she wails. I glance at the tape recorder I gave her. It looks like a toaster. All she needs to do is to post the tape into a slot, then press "play".

"Oh, Mother, there's no need to panic about that, don't worry about it!" I press the big red 'eject' button and out comes the cassette. I show it to her, then sit down next to her heavy armchair and take her hand, flashing with diamonds. It's still trembling.

"It's all fine, Mother. Tell me, what did you do today?"

"The shortbread that Audrey gave me, it's not the same as the Christmas shortbread."

"Are you saying that you ate some shortbread today, Mother?"

"Yes. At the day centre. Very crumbly. Too sweet. And I looked for the daffodils. But I couldn't see any. They've gone." I try to reassure her. "But they're in the stone trough on the wall. You said you saw them there yesterday."

"Yes. Yesterday, but where are they now? They've gone. Something has taken them."

"I saw them there too. They're already in flower. I'll go look for you."

It's difficult to see small daffodils in the half-dark, but there they are, flowering, scenting the evening air. When I return, Mother is pouring herself a stiff whisky, some of it slopping on to the table.

"I hope you can stay and talk to me for a while," she pleads, "I'm feeling a bit off today, haven't been out at all, the time does drag when you're on your own all day."

"But Mother, you've been to the day centre, you've just said that you had some shortbread there." She looks at me blankly. I continue: "I arranged for Audrey to collect you, and she must have done, because you've been talking about the shortbread." But Mother has already moved on.

"I'm really feeling rather full, don't much fancy any dinner, love," she adds. "Can we just have a little chat instead?" I don't enjoy these inconsequential conversations, and need to check for eggs before it gets too dark, then prepare the meal. But I'm concerned that she isn't hungry. I go into the kitchen to check the fridge.

"Mother? Did you put cream in your coffee today?"

"Yes, a little bit."

There's a large pot of double cream in there, and three quarters of it is gone. A milky spoon is lying next to it, on the fridge shelf, and some viscous white drips have puddled onto the floor.

"But Mother, you've eaten most of a carton of it. It's no wonder that you're not hungry and feel a bit 'off'." Again a blank stare. "I don't know what we're going to do when we run out of that cream," she says.

"Perhaps you shouldn't eat so much of it?"

"No, not that cream. The cream for putting on my head."

Outside the first bats are beginning to flicker through the rowan trees. They can only fly around here on these rare limpid evenings of no wind, when small insects rise from the pools and bogs. And the bullfrogs are calling, a curious, rhythmic rasp, as they seek for mates. I want to be out there: I've been indoors all day, and few evenings up here are as serene as this.

"Look, Mother," I say, standing up but still holding her hand, "There are things I need to do. It's getting dark now, soon I won't be able to see outside. If Adrian hasn't come home, I'll come and chat with you after I've finished."

"What things?"

I sigh. "Close in the chickens, dig up some leeks, make the meal-"

"But I don't want a meal. I'm not hungry today," says Mother.

"I know that. We've already discussed it, remember? But Adrian will want dinner. And I've a lecture to prepare for tomorrow too."

She takes another large slug of whisky, very slowly.

"What's the lecture about?"

I really want to end this conversation, just as much as she wishes to prolong it. Determined to cut her off, I answer, "Shifts in the Perception of Space in the Treatment of Landscape between Giorgione and Tintoretto."

Her eyes light up and she turns to me, putting down her tumbler. "Oh, how lovely! So that would include Titian, wouldn't it?"

I look at her in astonishment. "Yes, it does include Titian. How on earth would you -?"

"I remember it so well. Venice. All those years ago.

That amazing altarpiece, Santa Maria degli Frari. The Virgin. Ascending to heaven on a cloud, through such a blue sky. As though lit from within. You loved it. You were so excited."

"Yes," I say, putting down the egg basket.

"And then we went on to the Scuola di San Rocco. Tintoretto's frescoes there…" she adds.

I recall it clearly, this trip almost sixty years ago that determined my career. I was silenced by Venice, almost devoid of tourists at that date: echoing marble piazzas, reflected aqueous light illuminating the underside of carved cornices, walls of chalky ochre and madder against silky moving water, fretted in ironwork. Glittering mosaics in lacy cathedrals, the formality of Palladio's basilica frontages. My parents had taken the trouble to show me the glories of the High Renaissance at the age of seven. None of us really knew what we were looking at, but I spent my youth finding out. The clarity of Mother's distant memory amazes me.

"Mother? Would you like me to read you some of Father's diaries? I don't have them from then: but I do have the later ones."

"Oh yes! That would be really wonderful. It would bring it all back for me."

"Actually, Mother, you seem remarkably clear about it anyway."

"Sometimes, yes," she says, returning to the whisky, "but often not. I know I get confused. I just don't recognize when it's happening."

Oh, Lord. So she's realised that she's becoming demented. That terrible period, when her mind begins to fray and yet still she understands the inevitability of its impending loss. Maybe the diaries will keep it at bay? It's almost dark now, so I hurry to shut the pop-hole in the henhouse. Adrian would be cross if the fox got the chickens again, particularly if it's my fault. He should be home by now. After I've dug the leeks, I ring him.

"Yes?" he answers, "what's the matter?"

"You're normally home by now. I wondered if something's gone wrong."

"No. What's the problem?"

"Well, it's after eight now, and you haven't set off. You won't be back till nearly nine. It's already dark, you know."

"Oh yes," he says, "I hadn't realised the time. I've been trying to locate a bug all day, can't find it."

"So are you coming home, then?"

"I'll just start off one more simulation, then I'll leave it to run overnight and come back."

So he won't be leaving immediately, even now. There's time to find those diaries and read to Mother. I go up to the attic and unbuckle the dusty leather case containing my father's papers. Inside, among manila envelopes and hand-written certificates, are several small brown casebound notebooks, cream pages inside with red lines and blue margins. These are covered with his elegant cursive writing in fountain pen. I take one notebook at random: 'Holidays, August 1985 to April 1986.'

Mother is now mellow with whisky. I start to read to her. I flick through the diary, trying to locate a passage that isn't entirely about the weather.

Sept. 26th. A much better day and a nice run. After breakfast, (usual cornflakes and marmalade) there was warmish misty sunshine. We were away from the caravan by twenty seven minutes to ten. Straight up the hills from the middle of the village, making a left turn onto a narrow mountain very scenic road to Langholm. An interesting town, good Co-op, lots of ducks by the river and a really big useful car park. A Tibetan style monk in a dark red skirt! Then North on the A7 to Hawick, twelve and a quarter miles of very scenic route-

I put the notebook aside. "Mother, I don't think I can keep reading this to you. It's unbelievably boring, isn't it? Shall we try to find a more interesting bit?" Then I notice that her eyes are shut, her head leaning back against the tapestry cushion. "What's wrong?" I ask.

"Nothing," she says, the tears streaming down her face, "it's just wonderful. It's as if I can hear him speaking. He writes so beautifully, I can just imagine us back there in all those lovely places."

★

Later, when I put the diary back in the suitcase, I notice that underneath the notebooks is a bundle of folded foolscap paper, foxed with sepia patches. I open it carefully, some of the pages falling apart along the folds to reveal a less assured version of that same handwriting in faded pencil.

Saturday, June 30th 1934. The ride this scorching afternoon along the A5 road to Chester, newly sprayed with tar, which the occasional passing charabanc spattered onto my shorts, was alleviated by the genial company of the Cheshire Cycling Club out for a spin. After photographing the famous cathedral (really more like a roomy church, a great disappointment after York Minster!) we agreed to camp all together that evening. The Welsh hills beckoned, shimmering blue in the distance. We pitched our tents in the field behind the Colliers Arms at Tryddin. I hesitated to enter the hostelry in my khaki shorts and open necked shirt, but chalked on a slate outside was "Teas for cyclists", so I ventured within. They offered a plate of ham, pickled onion, bread and butter and lashings of sweet tea, it was delicious! My new companions soon joined me, and we could be found drinking earthenware jugs of cool cider long after closing time, brought out to us by the maid. It was warm and still light in the courtyard, and after we'd cracked a few jokes with her, the girl summoned the other barmaids. They were most impressed that we'd cycled more than a hundred miles that day! We all chatted and laughed far into the night, and more than one crept off to her companion's tent in the late gloaming….

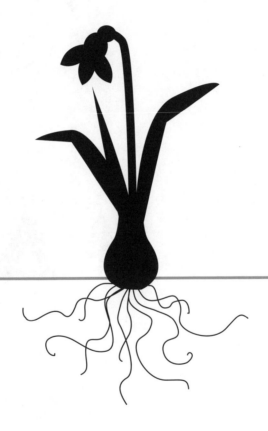

Mary Reval
The Prioress

Snowdrop time again, an early start
of spring. They spread across the grass like shreds
of lace. We planted them here where once our
cemetery was, hoping for eternal life.

My sisters buried in their shrouds, have long
ago merged into earth. Fast asleep,
they wait for the end of time to come.
For more than five hundred years, I rested

in my stone coffin in their midst until
I was taken away with my tomb
to make room for the sheep and their lambs.
They cemented the casket into the wall

of the priory. Now I have to stand
upright behind my funeral slab.
Sometimes, under a starless sky, I slip
out of my prison, glide over the field

to join all the others in the paddock.
Six of my flock are missing. They were sent
home to their families during King Henry's
dissolution, were interred far away.

The other day, there was an argument
in front of me between the woman who
made a garden next to me and a new
man who wanted to tear down my wall.

This would have made me a homeless
soul, a heap of old bones to be thrown away.
I heard the woman speak to the builders,
'The wall is haunted, because of the grave.

Don't touch.' The builders stepped back. It
gave me a bold idea. I summoned all my
remaining strength and dared to make
an appearance in the man's kitchen at night.

This did the trick. I'm now part of a listed
monument, the Keldholme wall. I still have
to stand in my box, but near my sisters.
Soon there will be new lambs in the paddock.

Dave Norman
Cassandra

There's nothing on the telly, it's the middle of the night, but my dad is sat there in his chair, staring at the screen. He doesn't even have the light on, there's only the flicker of Ceefax bathing his face with pixels.

He doesn't know I'm stood here watching him, worrying. I crept downstairs all careful but it wouldn't have mattered. He can't see or hear anything. Not me, not the telly. You'd think he was dead but then every now and then some instinct to stay alive reminds him to breathe… a deep, sad sigh, and he rubs his cheeks and eyes.

I want to help him. I want to hug him and be his little girl again. But then a voice I know so very well, a voice that only I can hear, gently whispers, "There's nothing you can do to help. You have to let him find his own way back…"

So I turn around and go back upstairs to bed. Because she's right.

Because she is always right.

When I get back from the doctors my mum is asleep with her head on the kitchen table. I make her a cuppa.

"I haven't done your dad's tea!" she splutters. She's been crying.

"It's alright, mum. He won't want to eat it anyway. I don't expect he's eaten his dinner yet."

"I'll re-heat it for him later. He's been alright today, your dad. Back to his usual self, talking about getting a job. He must have fell asleep and forgot to eat."

"Mum, you know that isn't…"

"True? Who knows what's really true?"

She doesn't know that I know someone who really does know what's really true. Who always knows the truth.

I pull my mum's head over to me and let it rest in my

lap. I stroke her careworn greying hair and smooth her eyebrows. Then we do our favourite thing and talk about the old house.

"You were only little then. It was a lovely house. It must have rained for some of the time but I don't remember it if it did. Your dad would spring up out of bed before the alarm clock went off and get himself ready to get off to work. Always laughing and making jokes about everything.

"He couldn't wait to see you in the mornings. I'd lie in bed and hear him come crashing in to see you and you'd be giggling, `Hello, Daddy`.

"And you never cried. We'd hear about other people having babies that kept them up all night with tears. Not you. You never cried. Later you did, but not then. Do you remember?"

Cassandra whispers in my ear, "Our picnics. We used to have picnics."

"I can only remember it a bit," I say. "I remember playing on the lawn."

"You'd sit out there for hours at a time and I'd worry if you were alright. I used to think you might want to go and play with the others but you wanted to be on your own. You had your little plastic tea set and you had little pretend tea parties. Gabbling away to yourself all afternoon. We might sit and watch you, Dad and me, or me and your Uncle Paul, 'Uncle Pom-pom', whoever was there at the time, and wonder, 'who's she talking to? whose she having her picnic with?

"Of course your father had his job then. That was before we had to come here..."

Then she remembers something.

"I never even asked you! What did the doctor say?"

"Not much," I tell her. "He never knows much. But I'll have to do some tests. It might not be just puppy fat after all."

For years I didn't even know her name. Names didn't worry us. After all, she didn't call me anything. We didn't need to call each other anything. Who else would we be talking to?

Then, when I learned her name, after everything that had gone on, I thought I don't even know what she looks like. She is my best friend and my only friend and I don't know what she looks like.

So I asked and she said, "I look like you, silly. Identical."

But for years I didn't even know her name, and of all places to actually learn something and learn something as important as that, I learnt it at school.

At the school that I hate; with the children that I hate and that hate me, that call me names because of how I look. With the teachers that I hate and that hate me; that call me names because of how I look.

There had been talk of some men fighting some old war and how one of the gods, the sun god or someone, fell in love with a young peasant woman while under the power of some old spell or something and in order to get her to go out with him he granted her a wish and the wish she asked for was the gift of Prophecy, which meant that she could see the way things were going to turn out in the long run. But when he started to get a bit too friendly she gave him the shove. He couldn't take back the gift but he made it so that whenever she tried to tell anyone the truth of what was going to happen before it even happened nobody would ever believe her. Until it was too late.

And

… her name was Cassandra.

And if her name was Cassandra, then her name was Cassandra.

So now I knew her name.

It was after we had moved to our new house, the one none of us liked as much, but a while before I found out her name. We were playing dressing-up in my mum and dad's bedroom because that was the best place to play it because it was where my mum's clothes all were and because she had a mirror, a big long mirror, taller than me, and if you turned the lights out and pulled the curtains shut you couldn't see the other houses and flats and could pretend you were somewhere good.

We looked at each other in that mirror a lot and talked about what might happen. She could always guess what things were next for us. She always came up with the best ideas for games (and always won) and had to show me how to make things work because I was clumsy and slow.

My mum had gone to the shops; it was the last chance she'd get. She hoped I didn't mind, she said she knew I'd be alright. My dad was looking after me, I liked that. Even though he cried a lot. Especially for a dad.

Water.

Blood.

I was wearing my summer dress and it was almost too small for me. And I had on my mum's posh shoes and even though I had big feet for a girl they were huge on me and I was wearing my mum's jewellery; her necklace and her rings and bracelets, a big belt of my dad's I'd found and his bright yellow woolly pom-pom hat.

Water!

Blood!

It was dark in the room but you could tell it was a sunny day through the curtains.

We had been playing but now we were talking. Serious.

We had been playing I Know Something You Don't Know but now it wasn't a game anymore. She really did know something I didn't know. She was trying to tell me but I couldn't understand. She was trying to tell me something was wrong, something had been wrong for a very long time but I was too stupid to understand. How could she make me understand?

Cassandra screamed.

Her scream filled my body. It did not stop.

Water! Blood!

Her scream filled my head and I didn't know what to do.

Water! Blood!

WATER!

BLOOD!

I punched the glass of the mirror and it broke and I ran away. But Cassandra was not in the mirror and her screams did not stop.

I ran into the living room to find my dad. He was gone. He's in the bathroom, silly. I called for him but he was gone.

Something's wrong. Wrong. Wrong! WRONG!

I ran into the street to find my dad.

Dad. Dad! Something's wrong...

There were men standing in the street, smoking cigarettes. They didn't seem to realise. If they did they didn't care.

There were women pushing prams. There were boys throwing stones at each other. Nobody budged an inch.

Nobody else could hear her.

Dad! Dad! There's something wrong! There's something wrong with our dad!

Tests.

And then more tests.

Then scans.

To find out what is wrong with me. Why I am the way I am.

I have been described as an interesting case. If one doctor or surgeon doesn't mind then another doctor or surgeon would like to have a peep beneath the covers.

Being in hospital is fairly bad but it's better than being at school. It smells of who knows what and no one knows or talks about what it is they've got. I suppose this must be what it's like to be a grown-up.

I am a grown-up now. Almost. I spent a long time in my mum and a long time as a little girl and now it seems I'm ready to be something else.

Someone who doesn't have Cassandra.

The night before she went we were very close. I didn't sleep.

She whispered in my ear, all giggly. "If it wasn't me then it would have been you. I would have been the pretty one; you would have been the brainy one. Or I would have been cleverer, you would have been prettier. It doesn't really matter, either way you'll forget me."

If I had shouted out that I would never forget her

and that I would never let her leave me then I would have woken up all the other girls in the ward, so I silently kissed her goodbye. I said it will only be goodbye until the morning, until after the operation then I promised I would try to find her. But she was getting ready to leave; she was so very tired from what the nurses had done, from the injections.

Then I thought of all our times together. I thought of how she always knew when something bad was coming. How she had told me that our little plastic teacups were not full of real tea. How she had tried to reassure me that the sheets stained with my bleeding were not a reason to be ashamed. How she had told me that my dad had never had a bright yellow pom-pom hat, somebody else must have left it there.

How she knew before I did that he had taken a razor to his throat and lain down in the hot water of the overflowing bath tub to put an end to all his misery.

How much I loved him. And my mum.

And my Dad's twin brother, Uncle Paul.

And my Mum's twin sister, Auntie Jean.

They had to cut me and detach the obstruction. Student doctors came to peer.

A lifeless clot of partly-formed hair and teeth and almost skin-and-bone.

The student doctors knew what she looked like. But I knew her name.

Vicky Morris
Meeting Margaret

I've told her to stay put
at the fountain, to just wait
until you see her and say, Margaret –
you'll know her by her beige anorak,
by her rounded shoulders, hunched
from years of stooping low
over sinks of holy water,
bleaching the everyday out of kitchen cloths
made from old vests and knickers,
over bath tubs, swirling together
The heavy fabric of three children
and an absent father.
You'll know Margaret
by her restless, disjointed shuffle,
forever trying to balance
in her own gravity.

And when you greet her,
don't mind if her smile is shy,
her teeth hidden;
she doesn't like to show
the gap her father left
at just thirteen.
Don't try to shake hands, she'll not want to.
She'll probably give you a clumsy hug,
turning her face away,
or clutch your arm
with hands so callused,
as a child, I'd try and catch her still,
for long enough
to touch the cracks
and marvel at the toughness
of human skin.

Vicky Morris
Mechanisms

He'd click his hair, my brother,
would sit in front of the TV,
curling a clump around fingers,
leaving one strand free
to hook under his nail and
pull across the coil like a bow
that snapped back -
his keratin knuckle crack.

I sucked my thumb,
would walk around the house
plugged into the comforts of mum;
her sanctuary before we met.
The appeasing suction of concave meets convex,
cocooned inside the womb of my mouth,
accompanied by the scratching of cloth.
At first a ribbon, like a violin,
moving calm against my nose,
then a blue polka-dot dress and over time,
scraps of other clothes. And then,
the prickles of adolescence;
the ceremony of letting go.

But still, my fingertips will always
seek out the right direction
in the fine rows of a soft polyester,
there is still something in its rubbing together
that induces relief
and sends me back
to once in a house of fires,
when I would smooth my charcoaled mind to sleep,
and the image of my sister
diverting the flames,
with her teeth across the knuckle of her index finger,
where I can still see the scar.

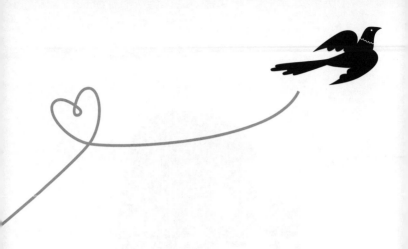

Virginia Lowes
Let Us Speak of Such Things

'Can you fix that curtain, Sam?' She jerked her head towards one end of the delicate daisy print fabric.

'Well I've left it like that…'

'I know why you've left it, but can you fix it?' Hazel interrupted sharply.

'But I don't want our little vermin friends to see me.'

'O for God's sake, you're not Davey Crockett.' Her chair scraped the floor.

It had come early this year. Time to batten down the hatches, he thought as she began to clear the table. Hazel lifted his cup and spilled tea on the page of adverts he was reading. He didn't react.

'I'll wash up,' he said, instead.

'OK.'

She washed her hands slowly at the sink, then stared at the 28 days of February on the wall calendar as she dried each finger, and her hands, front and back.

He skimmed the classifieds: permanent hair reduction; skip hire; loft storage solutions; vertical, roller and roman blinds; 3-piece suites; divan beds and plain, patterned or traditional concrete paving. He thought he might get a quote on the paving, just to keep his eye on the competition.

He picked up the rest of the crockery from the table and carried it to the sink where Hazel had left the dirty plates and cutlery. He rinsed it all off under the cold tap then watched her in the garden as the plastic washing up bowl filled with hot soapy water. She was carrying her cushion wrapped in a plastic bag, and the trug crammed with a trowel, fork, gloves, snippers, string and seed packets.

He'd already got his potatoes chitted, and seedlings started nicely in the greenhouse; peas and beans, celeriac and cabbage. They were all pretty self-sufficient once they got started. He hadn't time to nurture.

Most of the year Hazel said nothing when he loaded
his rifle with pellets and took pot shots at pigeons and
rats scavenging outside, so they had compromised. The
times that this bleakness descended upon her, he put the
gun away. He knew the thought of anything losing its life
tortured her, as if it were her own existence threatened.

The window overlooked an ornate garden. At the bottom,
just before his vegetable patch, were gooseberry, raspberry
and blackcurrant fruit bushes that would produce heavily
come the late summer. Roses, not quite budding yet,
clambered over an arched trellis at the path entrance
where stone slabs ran, slightly off centre, down the length
of the garden. This side of the fruit was a knot garden.
Hazel didn't like Sam to touch this. It was a low neatly
pruned hedge of three pentagons, planted with herbs
and flowers. She kept it pristine, unlike other areas of
the garden where she seemed to encourage disorder
and chaos. He'd seen her sprinkle seeds from a height,
letting the wind carry them to a resting place. Or find an
unlabelled packet in her pocket, "I'm sure these are sweet
peas," she had said, and prodded them into the soil.

He turned off the tap and saw she was sitting at the
wooden table halfway down the garden. They would
get through this. They always did. They just had to sit
it out, support each other. It usually lasted a week and
it was only once a year. Sam tried to be around for her,
but to keep himself busy at the same time. She'd been
talking about a lot of the pot plants being rootbound and
it looked like she'd collected them together with some
bigger pots.

One year the whole garden had been red all year round.
That was the year after they lost Briony, after nine
months in the womb. Hazel had worn red outfits for the
whole year too. When people asked why she was always
wearing red, she would say it was because she had lost

her daughter, who had lived and was full of healthy blood right up until that moment when she should have come out into the world screaming, but somewhere in those last few hours her little heart had stopped beating. Of course most people were uncomfortable with this answer. And even when she abbreviated it to, "I lost my daughter this year, and I want to think about her," the responses were no more encouraging.

'That's only natural,' he said when she returned from work crying. He stroked her hair, and found a clean handkerchief to wipe her mascara and tears. It was her second day back in the office after three months off sick. 'People never know what to say about a death.'

'They could say something,' she shook with anger. He hugged her. 'She's our daughter; we can't expect other people to understand.'

'I don't want understanding or pity or even sympathy. I want acknowledgement. I want to be able to talk about that part of my life instead of it being skirted around as if it's something shameful. I haven't committed a crime. I didn't even have any choice in it.'

'I know my darling. We're on the same side.'

They had gone to the woodland burial site that evening and planted bulbs by the wooden memorial plaque which read: "Our Darling Briony. Nine months in our lives. Always in our hearts."

Their tears had soaked into the soil.

'I'm in a no-woman's land,' Hazel had said once, 'I didn't need a little blue line to tell me I was pregnant. I felt my body already preparing to stretch, curve, fill out, to create a sanctum. I was nurturing our child. I was a mother.' He smiled sadly at her. 'I know I'm still a mother even though our child is dead. But when other parents are talking about their children, I can't share those experiences I had, or the love I feel for Briony.' She paused. 'Don't you feel like that?' He was thoughtful.

'Now and again, I suppose. But to be honest it's not the sort of conversation I have very often. Have you got

another counselling session?' She looked at the calendar,
    'Tomorrow night. I'll talk to her about it.'

Life had moved on but the answer to the innocuous,
"Have you got any children?" was never easy. It was
an opening to talk about Briony, but on the whole,
the lowered eyes, sideways glances and shuffling feet,
embarrassed Hazel. Eventually she made excuses not to
meet new people and the garden took on more and more
significance.
    By the following April, twelve months of counselling
sessions had come to an end. As had Hazel's red
wardrobe. The garden had been planted white, and the
following year violet.

They visited Briony's burial site on her birthday and
whenever their grief engulfed them. When it rained they
were sheltered by the treetop canopy and they would
count growth rings on the dead fall or trace the tough
ring of a knot where a branch had once been connected.
They found comfort in the soft sounds their footfall
made in the bracken and leaves and the smell of the
damp woodland earth.

He made himself a coffee and opened his mail. He
had two cheques for work he'd finished. Two private
houses, one had been building a small fish pond and
the other making some raised beds for a gardener now
in a wheelchair. He took pride in his work, using local
and recycled timber, hiring tools from the small garden
centre that sent work his way. It was a good arrangement,
he hadn't been out of work since... since that month he'd
allowed himself to grieve with Hazel.

It was only at this time, when he needed to be with her,
when he couldn't be busy, that he also felt the sadness.
He stood up to stretch and took a sip of his bitter coffee.
Through the window he noticed that Hazel had gone
from the garden, and, as he placed his cup on the table
he saw the burnt golden blur of a cock pheasant glide

into the garden. The feathers gleamed in soft sunlight, the crimson face in stark contrast to the dark naked branches of the surrounding trees.

Without a second thought Sam moved silently and stealthily to the utility room, picked up his loaded .22 rifle and returned to the spot just behind the window where the curtain hung down. With the butt steadied against his shoulder he carefully placed his left hand beneath the forestock of the gun, and his right beneath the trigger guard. Automatically his finger curled around to its natural position on the trigger. He squinted through the optic, located the pheasant and zoomed up to a nine times magnification. His heart thudded like a jackhammer as he thought of the pleasure of pulling the trigger, of hearing the bang, of feeling the recoil through his whole body. He remembered the sweet pleasure of dining on a bird he'd shot, plucked and roasted himself. He recalled the cloudy night he was finally invited to go lamping with his father and One Eyed Tom; downwind, he aimed the beam of the torch along the hedge lines. The moment he caught the glint of a rabbit, One Eyed Tom shot, and his father ran over to pick it up. That had been the first of many such nights.

He tightened his finger on the trigger just as he heard Hazel's footsteps on the stairs. He hesitated, looked again through the optic, squared it up, the bird was perfectly still. His finger twitched, then he drew the gun in, and silently replaced it in the utility. He returned to the kitchen window and hung the curtain back on the rail. She stood beside him and peered out. 'There's a pheasant outside. It's beautiful.'

'I know.' He kissed her cheek. She took his hand, 'I've just done a pregnancy test.' She felt his hold tighten. 'It's blue. We're going to have a second baby.' Outside, with a great beating of air, the bird flapped into the pale spring sky and flew away.

Suzanne McCardle
Extract from the novel Bone Lake:
Art students Bridie and Antonio discovered her nanny
Patti's remains on a trip to France.

The first Saturday night at college Antonio invited
me to his room. He lived two floors up in the Hall of
Residence. It was rumoured that the block was based
on the design of a Swedish women's' prison, and I could
believe that – the rooms were no bigger than cells – with
their hard, built-in sleeping platforms, and just enough
scope to shimmy between bed, desk and wardrobe.
In between each pair of rooms was a bathroom, with
doors on either side. You had to remember to lock your
neighbour's door rather than your own. Again, everything
was crammed into the smallest amount of space. The
shower was above the toilet, and, until we remembered
to move it out of the way, my toilet-sharer and I had a
very soggy loo roll.

The first thing I saw in Antonio's room was the
collection of bones on the window sill, carefully laid out,
and mirroring my own. This seemed to be yet more proof
that somehow we belonged together.

'When did you start collecting?' I asked.

'I'm not weird or anything.' Antonio stood in front
of the window, shielding the small display from my view.
'No! They're beautiful – the lines. I like to draw them. I
collect, too.' His shoulders relaxed and he stood sideways
allowing me in to look at his treasures.

'These are just the smaller ones,' he said. He had
commonplace, but still beautiful, skulls from a rabbit,
a fox, and various birds which I recognised from my
own collection, but he also had a short-eared owl and a
fruit bat, which I didn't have. We talked bone stripping
techniques as Antonio produced a bottle of red wine.

We drank quickly. Antonio pulled another from

under the bed and refilled our tumblers. We were lying on the narrow bed, heads resting on the pillow. Both of us were tipsy. Antonio turned and I could smell garlic and wine on his breath.

'If only you were a boy!' Antonio sighed, looking deep into my eyes. 'You'd be perfect.'

'If only you were a man!' I giggled, tipping my beaker and spilling red wine onto the duvet. 'You'd be perfect. Not that you're not a man. You know what I mean.' I think we both leaned forward for the kiss. It was soft and experimental. And then we both drew away. I didn't have much experience of kissing. I had practised on the back of my hand in readiness, and once my best friend and I had tried a snog, but we couldn't see anything great about it, and this experience with Antonio was similar; chaste, sexless, unexciting.

'Nah, you don't have the right equipment,' he said, shaking his head, 'it won't work.' I wasn't sure if equipment, or the lack of it, was the reason the kiss was so underwhelming. Because we were drunk there wasn't the embarrassment I would have normally felt. 'Here, I got you something.' Antonio dived under the bed and brought out a bright orange supermarket carrier. He spread out a slightly musty, purple lace dress. It was nipped in at the waist with layers of net beneath the skirt. 'Put it on.' I peeled off my leggings and tunic and stepped into the dress. Antonio zipped up the back of it and then thrust me away from him as I imagined a mother might look at her growing daughter. Luckily the skirt was long and hid most of my bare white legs.

'Let me do your face to match.' Antonio pulled out another carrier with a selection of brand new make-up. 'I started work today,' he said, 'flogging false eyelashes and doing mini make-overs.' He worked on me expertly, matching my lips to the dress. Then he went to his wardrobe and produced a purple hairband with butterflies. He arranged this on my head and then showed me the result in the mirror.

'Did you make this?' I asked. Antonio nodded. 'You're good!'

'I know.' I looked hard and glossy, pretty much how I felt. I had had to protect myself with a decorative veneer for most of my life. I put on my Doc Martens as Antonio dressed in a sharp suit with a dicky bow topped off with a bowler hat.

'Shall we?' he said, offering me his arm.

He walked me to a nice hotel, all the while evading my questions about where we were going.

'I haven't got much money!' I said, seeing the plush looking exterior and the fancy cars. Dad had refused to contribute to my education, so everything was on student loans, and the amount I was getting was pretty much swallowed up by the cost of my room. I had to work to eat, never mind party. Antonio waved this away telling me that the evening would be cheap, so, lured by the idea of cheap, I went inside. We followed the noise of a disco and entered a room decked out for a wedding. 'Whose is the wedding?' I asked. I could see that it wasn't a student crowd. These were normal people; folk with mortgages, whose children were playing hide and seek under the tables. Still it was possible that Antonio had run into them somewhere; perhaps he'd met the bride (or groom) at work. My question was almost drowned out by the music, and ignored by Antonio, who was already heading for the present table. Not to leave one, but to check out the names on the gift cards. It was at that point that I realised. A couple came and placed a parcel on the table. I smiled at them tensely. 'Whose wedding is this?' I repeated. Antonio tilted one of the gift cards. It read 'Fergus and Finola'.

'An alliterative couple as it turns out,' Antonio commented. 'Come on let's grab some food and alcohol!' The couple were still hovering by the table. The woman smiled at me.

I moved my cheeks and mouth, attempting a smile back, before turning to Antonio and asking hoarsely, 'Can we speak outside?' I hauled him into the corridor. 'We can't just join a stranger's party!'

'It'll be fine. Everyone will assume that we belong to the other side. No one will ask. Trust me. Just don't talk

to the bride and groom together.' I stared at Antonio.
It was a scary idea to me, to blag your way through
something; to pretend to be someone you weren't, but I
could feel myself swithering. Perhaps it reminded me of
the games Patti and I used to play – that childish mix of
excitement you get from pushing boundaries – I felt that
I had lived a very dull life so far, and I wanted to be more
exciting, to have some of Antonio's glamour. 'What else
are we going to do?' Antonio asked. I pictured the rest of
the evening back in Halls – watching TV – going to bed
at eleven. Just like my life had been before at boarding
school; regimented. I wanted to break out.

'Okay!' We went back in and I followed Antonio's
lead, hoovering up egg sarnies and mushroom
vol-au-vents and discarded drinks.

This became our standard Saturday night out, if I
wasn't working at the pub. We switched hotels, never
visiting the same one two weeks in a row, so the staff
didn't become suspicious.

After the wedding we found a party. There was
always a party somewhere; sometimes fellow students,
sometimes young professionals. That first evening the
first party we came upon was filled with young men in
shiny shirts, and women in belt-length skirts. We stood
out straight away like albino rabbits in the wild, but by
then we were both pretty drunk and Antonio went as far
as finding out the name of the host, expertly pumping
the first guy we met in the hallway for details. The host
was Doug and he worked in IT for the council.

Antonio shook his head. I think he thought that
Doug sounded boring, and his instincts told him to move
on, so we wavered along the street, until we saw another
open doorway with music, and a more studenty-looking
crowd spilling out onto the pavement. I watched Antonio
lock eyes with a guy across the room. They were a similar
height, and their mouths curved in the same way, but this
guy was dressed in jeans and a tight T-shirt.

'He's coming over!' he squealed. 'Look, if I don't see you
later, call me tomorrow!' And with that I was alone again.

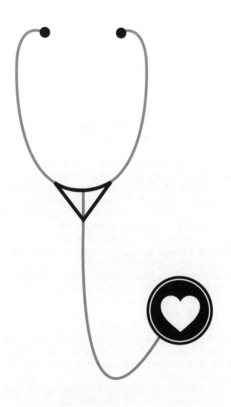

'Hey, beautiful!' I didn't know if the guy was taking the mickey, but the alcohol had softened me, and I was ready for that veneer to be penetrated. Antonio melted away. The man who thought I was beautiful leaned over me. I had my back against the wall. He was tall with dark curling hair. His nose was crooked, as if it had been broken. 'So, where have you been hiding?' he asked. I laughed. Such a corny line. And then he kissed me, cutting off my laughter. This was a different kiss; it was full of insistent chemicals, and my lips, which had never been kissed like that before seemed to take on a life of their own. 'I'm a medical student,' he breathed in my ear. 'Do you want to see my stethoscope?'

Later I had his stethoscope slung around my neck, swinging between my bare breasts.

'Stay!' he murmured, waking as I crept from the bed. The house carpets were sticky. I had lain awake, listening to the sound of a stranger's breathing, and suddenly all I wanted to do was get out of there. I dressed quickly and walked the dark pavements back to Hall where I slept until lunchtime. I felt grubby when I woke up and began to remember what had happened. But this was student life, wasn't it? I was meant to hook up and have fun. I ran the shower, soaking the toilet roll.

Antonio came knocking and we made coffee in my shared kitchen at the end of the corridor. We took the drinks back to my room and curled up on the bed sipping them. Antonio couldn't stop grinning.

'How was your date?' I asked.

'Fine,' he said. He leaned back against the wall with his eyes closed and a self-satisfied smile playing on his lips. He opened his eyes and looked at me suddenly. 'How was your night?'

'Great!' I said it too brightly. He touched my hair. 'I'm sorry I took off. You didn't mind that I left you?'

'No. No, of course not.' Perhaps I should have minded, but up until this point being left by people was my default position, and I had crept away from Mr Stethoscope in the dead of night without leaving a number.

Rebecca McCormick
Weed Whacking in a Fedora

My husband did the garden in a worn-out felt fedora
Pulled down low over his brow which gave his face a frown.
He mowed the lawn in neat little stripes
As if trimming the pitch at Anfield or Stamford Bridge
Brought out the strimmer with its orange wire trailing
It would start up with a wail,
The high-pitched thrum of a suburban Sunday.

Everyone said how beautiful his lawns were
Their pretty borders all neatened
Bright flowers standing tidily in clumps awaiting
Inspection from a perfectionist's eye
He took such care over his yards that it was sort of a shame that
There was nothing left for me.

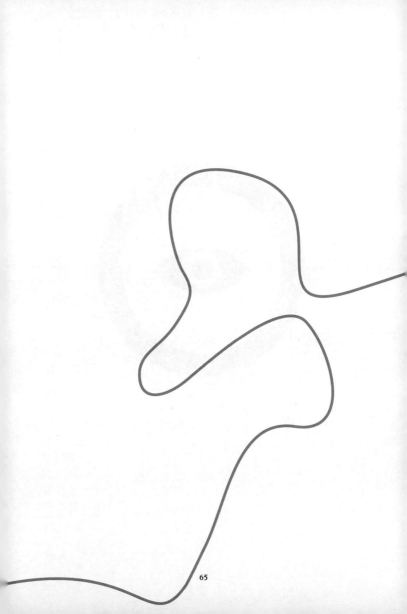

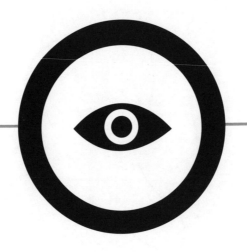

Rebecca McCormick
Film Directors in Mexico

They arrived in big cars seven
At a time, they stomped
Over our land, kicking mud
From the yard
I would not let them in the house
They spoke to my husband in stilted Spanish
Gesturing at me
Miming a film
They bought groceries as directed
I started to cook
Mixing, kneading, rolling, measuring
They stood around, hand on hips
Looking through their machines
All lidless eyes on me
They made me up, pulled at my clothes
Asked me to start again
Sweat dripped from under my bonnet
They motioned at me to smile
I tried, I really did.

Steve Emmerson
12 Years
(a five-minute play)

CHARACTERS – middle-aged couple – Carol and Neil
PROPS – Rag doll and a music box (see hyperlink-note later!)

North of England, tonight.

On stage – a small bed – empty except for a rag doll. Beside
the bed – a small music box.
Stage dark. Noises off – Neil and Carol are drunk –

NEIL:	*[Singing]* …Oh-oh Carol!
CAROL:	In bed.
NEIL:	I am but a fo-oo-ool…
CAROL:	In bed.
NEIL:	Darlin' I love you…
CAROL:	In bed.
NEIL:	Though you treat me crooooooool…
CAROL:	In bed.
NEIL:	You hurt me…
CAROL:	In bed.
NEIL:	And you make me cry-y-y…
CAROL:	In bed.
NEIL:	But if you leave me…
CAROL:	In bed.
NEIL:	I will surely die-ie-ie…
CAROL:	In bed.
	They collapse into drunken laughter.

CAROL: 'Appy birthday, love.

NEIL: 'Appy birthday...

CAROL: It's not my birthday.

NEIL: Well 'appy bloody Friday, then...

CAROL: *(Raucous laughter.)* It's not even bloody Friday...

          Shared drunken laughter again.

CAROL: Ey... Ey...

NEIL: What?

CAROL: Ey...

NEIL: What?

          Quiet... A bit more quiet...

CAROL: *(More serious now.)* How we gonna finish yer birthday, then?

NEIL: Well gimme a minute to think about it...

CAROL: What's to think about?

          A bit more quiet...

CAROL: You ready?

NEIL: Yea... You?

CAROL: Just a minute...

          A bit more quiet... Neil appears on the edge of the stage, looking across at the small bed. He switches on the light. The bed and rag doll alone are illuminated. Neil is shadow stage-left.

          Pause.

          Neil approaches the bed, picks up the doll, gazes at it.

          Pause.

          He tucks in the doll and picks up the music box.

          Pause.

NEIL: You ... should be asleep.

DOLL:

NEIL: Way past yer bed time, little lady.

DOLL:

NEIL: Ok. Just once. Then sleep.

           *Neil winds the music box and we get
           Mozart's Magic Flute.*

           Pause.

NEIL: Told yer! Just once…

DOLL:

NEIL: All right! All right! One more time then it's
           definitely time for light out. Right?
           Definitely…

           Neil winds the music again box.

           Pause.

           Noises off – drunken singing –

CAROL: Oh-oh Carol, I am but a foo-oo-ool, darlin'
           I love you, though you treat me–

           Pause.

CAROL: Neil?

           Pause.

           Neil lowers his head, the music box still in his hands.

           Pause.

           Carol appears stage left in shadow.

CAROL: Ne-il?!

NEIL:

           Carol remains in the background, in the shadow.

CAROL: Come on love… It's yer birthday…

NEIL: Am comin'…

CAROL: Come on…

NEIL: One minute.

           Pause.

CAROL: Not tonight, love…

71

NEIL: No different to any other night…

CAROL: It's yer birthday… We promised…

NEIL: I know. I'll only be a minute.

Pause.

CAROL: Twelve years, Neil… Can't you– ?

NEIL: –Twelve years… Might as well be twelve days– Twelve hours–

Pause.

CAROL: I'm goin' to get in bed. In twelve minutes the light goes out an' yer birthday's gone… Okay…?

NEIL: Okay.

CAROL: Twelve minutes.

NEIL: Yea.

Carol departs. Neil remains beside the bed.

DOLL:

NEIL: Way past… You should 'a been asleep hours ago, young lady…

DOLL:

NEIL: Once! Okay… One more time and that's it. I mean it this time. Okay?

Music box. Magic Flute.

Neil picks up the doll. Holds it to his chest. Lowers his head.

Fade light as the music box winds down.

END

The Music Box:
www.youtube.com/watch?v=roakaYKHEy4

Simon Bestwick
As White as Bone

Halfway round the lakeshore path, Anne started to cry. At first I didn't hear; the squelch of boots in muddy earth and the huff of our breathing masked a lot. There was some distant traffic on the motorway, too. That helped drown it out, as well. Or maybe I just didn't want to hear.

But when I finally heard the first snuffles, I couldn't pretend they were anything else. I glanced across the lake – I was nearest the edge of the path, with the best view of it. The blue sky above it was very clear, the dull-coloured water gleaming all from the shore to the island at its centre. She might stop of her own accord, in a moment. Anne hated making a scene in public, even though the park was virtually empty. There was a man coming in the opposite direction, but that was all. I didn't know quite what to do till she began to sob.

Her eyes were red. Tears ran down her cheeks. Either she'd been crying longer than I'd thought, or harder; either way I was a bastard taking so long to react.

"Oh Max," she blubbered - it's the only word for it, her lips trembled and flapped like damp cloth on a line, grief the wind that blew it. "Max –" Scenes in public be hanged; I hugged her. The walker glanced at us in passing. I watched his retreating back, daring him to look round, intrude again. Perhaps he felt it, because he didn't. A muffled animal cry tore out of her. I shushed her, rocked her, but nothing could make it right.
We'd come here countless times in the past. When we'd moved here, thirty-odd years ago, newly-wed and planning a family, we'd been delighted to discover it. Affordability and a decent area to raise a child had been our priority. But to find a big country park – converted from the site of a former colliery – complete with a lake –

well, that'd put the tin lid on it.

Time was we came here almost every day, but this was our first visit since Peter drowned. It'd been over a month.

So many good memories, attaching to this place – you'd think they'd help balance out the bad. But they couldn't. Like the one bad apple, soiling the rest of the barrel; you can't reclaim the ground. It's like betrayal – the old rules can't apply, the old trust. The wounds hurt. They reopen periodically. They do not, ever, heal.

No-one can survive the death of a child. Who had told me that? Arthur Bryan, that was it, an older man I'd worked with, long retired and moved to Devon with his second wife. When his first wife died, they'd been separated for years. They'd lost a child; I didn't even know the sex, let alone the circumstances, only that it'd died. That, and that the loss had spelt the end of their marriage. Kids are notoriously inquisitive – Peter was so curious as a boy, if you didn't watch him he'd slip out and run across the main road to explore. God, the worry of that. Perhaps Arthur or his wife'd taken their eyes off the kiddie for the wrong minute, and –

Or maybe it'd just been the loss. You don't expect to bury your child. It's just wrong. An aberration.

"It's alright, love," I told her, patting her hair. She sniffed, nodded – although of course it wasn't alright, it could never be – and straightened up. "Come on," she said.

"Are you sure?"

"Yes." She closed her eyes, breathed out. "Sorry, love," she said, patting my arm. "Got a hanky?" I passed one over. She dabbed her face. "Is my mascara alright?"

"It's run a little," I said.

"Oh." She dabbed at it. "Never mind. Come on." As if I'd been the one holding things up.

We'd reached the place. Now we left the path and picked our way down the sloping ground to the water's edge.
We stopped at a small, shallow inlet. It looked pretty; a child might fish here for stickleback or baby roach with a jamjar. All sign of Peter's death was wiped away.
Anne'd been carrying a bunch of flowers with her all the

way about the lakeshore. Now she half-crouched but hovered, not knowing, it seemed, where to put them. In the end, she divided the bunch in two. Half she laid at the edge of the inlet; the rest she pitched out, scattering into the water, as if throwing bread to ducks.

I made a move towards her, but she waved me back. Now I hovered. Stooped like that, she looked as if she might be sick, but she didn't. Instead she cocked her head and said,

"What?"

"Love?" I called, and she waved me back again, seemed about to speak once more. But she didn't. She only grew still and straightened up. She hugged herself, looking out across the lake towards the island. "Love?" I asked again. "Are you alright?"

"I'm fine," she said, voice brittle and dull. "Thought I heard something, that's all." There was a silence; still she didn't turn towards me. A heron flew over the island, long wings slowly beating. "Do us a favour, love? Just leave me a minute or two. Just for a bit. Alright?"

"OK," I said. She said nothing else; I clambered back up the slope to the path. I stood looking down at her for a bit. There was a bench a few yards down. I went to it and sat, because my knees hurt, and waited for her.

★

It started that night. We went home, and I cooked a meal, while Anne sat in the living room, ignoring the TV's babble, and looking at old photo albums. There was Peter as a baby, a toddler; Peter in his first school uniform. Peter at University, at graduation, just before it began to go wrong. There were not many pictures of him after that. Just a few, from when the voices in his head had gone away for a while, and the side-effects of the anti-psychotics weren't as bad. He'd gained weight, was pale and slow-moving; found it hard, often, to speak properly. We had loved him, but even so. I wondered if Anne, when she'd heard Peter had walked into the lake at the park, his pockets full of stones – if she'd felt the same guilty relief. Perhaps. But I doubt she acknowledged it, even to herself.

We ate, we went to bed. I went to hold her but she turned away. Space, cold air, seemed to divide us. I wondered if this was the beginning of the end, if our child's death was ending us too, and stared up at the ceiling, miserable with guilt and loss, till I drifted off. I woke in the early hours of the morning, and knew I was alone and something wrong. The bed was empty; the house was cold. The wind was blowing outside, and seemed louder than it should be. When I the front door banged, I leapt out of bed.

I keep a poker under the bed, just in case. You hear such stories, about burglars. And perhaps there'd always been the niggling fear that Peter – but that was silly, I knew. The mentally ill, in fact, are rarely violent. At times it might've been easier if he had been. The paranoia, the compulsive behaviour. It'd worn us down, me down, the exhausting, frustrating business of tending someone who lived in a subtly different, grotesque other world from us, but in the same house.

I investigated, poker in hand, turning lights on as I went, but the house was empty. I shut the door and locked it, wondering how it'd got open. Only then did I realise Anne wasn't only not in bed, but not in the house. I was dialling the police when she banged on the door and called my name. I let her in; she was in her dressing gown, her slippers muddy, and she was frozen and shivering. "Anne, where have you been?" I asked. She felt stiff and cold. "Make me a cup of tea, Max," she whispered. So I did. My own hands were shaking as I did. Thinking how I'd lost a son to madness, and might now be about to lose my wife too.

*

It happened again the following night. I didn't know what to do. I watched by the window. After an hour or so, I saw her come back up the road in her nightclothes. They were stained with mud again. She didn't seem to see me. I climbed back into bed and pretended to be asleep when she joined me. But I wasn't, and lay awake long after she'd drifted off, staring at the ceiling again. She'd come from the direction of the country park.

I wasn't going to lose her too. There'd been warnings with Peter; he'd tried to walk into the lake before. Said it was calling him. That there was treasure down there, in the deep, enough to keep us all for life. No need to work again. If he could just get down there. Hence the stones. To weight him down. He'd been caught at it before, stopped. But you can't watch all the time.

★

The third night, I followed her. I hadn't been able to sleep anyway, so I just feigned it, waiting for her, and at last she moved, slipping out of bed, donning slippers and dressing gown, only just cleaned.

I heard the floorboards creak in the hall, the front door open. After a moment, I climbed out of bed, quickly dressed and followed.

I knew where she was going. This late there was no-one else on the street. She turned off down the steep road towards the park. In the clear moonlight, I could see the lake gleaming in the distance.

There are no gates at the park. There's a stone bridge you have to pass under, and then you just follow a long, straight path to reach the lake. She was easy to see in the dark.

The night was clear, the moon full. Silver light glowed on the grass each side of the long path, past the shuttered ranger station. She never looked back; before long I wasn't even trying to follow surreptitiously. She reached the small wooden platform overlooking the lake. I couldn't begin to count the times we'd come here over the years, but never in the dark. It was a new world; the lake, utterly still, shone like silvered glass, and the trees on the far side were black, jagged and spiky, like the dark woods of a children's fairy tale. I couldn't decide if the island looked romantic now, or sinister... Anne stood looking out across it for some time, hands resting on the

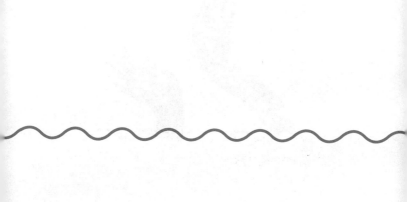

wooden handrail, surrounded by loose feathers and duck and goose excrement, then turned and moved away, onto the footpath that led around the shore, where she'd cried and I'd comforted her three mornings ago.

I followed her; she came off the path and down to the inlet. The withered remains of her flowers were still there. She knelt, bowed her head, rocked to and fro.

After a moment, when I could hear her start to weep, I came down the slope, softly calling her name. She didn't turn around. I reached her side. "Anne?" I said, and reached out. "Darling, what are you –?"

She turned then, brought the poker out from under the dressing gown and landed it across my shins. I heard bone crack; the pain was an instant later in coming and I opened my mouth to scream as I fell forward, but I landed face-first in the water and it was cut short. I couldn't stand. Anne advanced, swinging again; all I could do was scramble backwards in the water. She swung once more, clipping the supplicating hands I'd raised. I screamed aloud then, and startled birds took flight.

You can know a face twenty-odd years and it can still become one you've never seen before. She was crying – I'd seen that before, of course – but she'd never shown me hatred before; it made her face something else, a mask.

"He told me," she said. "Peter told me, you evil – you evil bastard. He told me what you did." I'm not evil, I wanted to say. I didn't – I just couldn't bear anymore. "He whispered in my ear, told me to act as if I couldn't hear him. Let you think you'd got away with it."

That first time we'd come here, after the drowning. "What?" she'd said. Then how still she'd gone. And stiff when I tried to hold her. "You told him to fetch the treasure," she said. "You let him out that evening, when I was away. You even told him about the stones." A night like this. A cloudless sky; a full moon, white as bone. "You told him to put stones in his pockets. How could you? How could you? Your own son." The pain of putting up with him, of endurance. Like water on stone, wearing it down, drip by bloody drip. And when we were gone, what of him then?

She screamed and swung wildly; I flailed backwards

with my broken legs, and suddenly I was fighting to keep
my head above water. It was up to Anne's thighs, and I
was several yards further out. And couldn't stand. She
lowered the poker, smiling.

"Peter?" she said.
Water slopped behind me, displaced by the movement
of something large and heavy.

No. It couldn't be him. Peter had been cremated.
They'd fished him out of the lake and cremated him.
It couldn't be him. I told myself that right up until my
son took my head in his hands and drove it beneath the
surface of the lake.

Much later, it seemed, I watched him and my wife
limp away through the dark. I stayed in the water, of
course. I'm still there now. Bodiless and lost, in the
mirrorlike, silvered glass of the lake. Beneath a moon as a
white as bone.

Linda Hartley
Doggerland

*The words of his mouth were smoother than butter, but war
was in his heart: his words were softer than oil, yet were they
drawn swords. ~Psalms 55:21*

London 1980

She lay in bed staring through the gap in the curtains at
the blue sky. At least she could see the sky here unlike
the basement where instead of curtains a heavy metal
grill covered the window that faced out onto a grim box-
like courtyard with a roof of black bars. Rachel lay there
like she used to, unable to think of a good reason to get
up, but she forced herself up all the same. Opening the
curtains she stared down at the Chelsea Avenue lined
with trees and posh boutiques. Up here on the tenth
floor, all life below seemed alien, as if it was happening a
great distance away.

She showered and dressed before making tea. The
apartment was silent apart from the chink of her teacup
as she placed it back in its saucer. She switched on the
hairdryer and blasted the silence away, pulling hard on
the hairbrush to straighten out her curls. Straight hair
made her look older than seventeen and when she stared
at her painted reflection she thought she could easily pass
for twenty. She never used to wear make up. She thought
it was showing off. With him though it was different.
She read to pass the time, stories by Danielle Steele
about young girls in dire circumstances who managed
to escape. She knew it was sentimental slush, but they
lightened her spirits, gave her hope. Today, however,
she couldn't concentrate and placed the book down on
the sofa beside her curled up feet. The apartment was
compact; yet had everything she needed. The kitchenette

with its hotplate and fridge was sufficient, for when he came they either went to a restaurant, or ordered food in. She liked the word apartment, it sounded more grown up and exotic than flat. After all, this was no tatty basement but Nell Gwynn House, the art deco block whose foyer smelt of leather and polish and had a porter in a grey uniform and a revolving glass door

Pasha didn't force her to stay inside, there was no lock on the door and yet she rarely went out. She missed working at the club. She missed the other girls. Sometimes she thought if only there was someone to talk to. Her parents were still angry with her for running away. More so since she'd started seeing Pasha. 'You should be with people your own age. Don't you see you are missing out.' She couldn't see, and they couldn't explain. Pasha loved her completely; in a way she had always wanted to be loved, but never felt before. And yet she felt uneasy as if each day she were moving a little further apart from everything, a little further apart from herself.

Last week she summoned up the courage to tell him that sometimes she was afraid to go outdoors. He looked at her strangely and she was afraid he would think her mad.

'Of course there's nothing the matter. In any case what do you need to go outside for, I'll get you anything you need.' She'd never seen him so happy, fussing around her and giving her firm orders not to leave the bed while he fried her a steak, passing her magazines, chocolate anything he thought might please her.

Later, she watched TV whilst he sat crossed legged on the floor and laid out his cards. He read all kinds of things into the hearts, diamonds, spades and clubs. He believed the cards contained secrets. Secrets he couldn't fathom, such as why Persia, the country he left as a boy, had fallen into the hands of Islamic fundamentalists?

'My sister is being forced to wear the chador' he said, 'she has never worn it in her life. When I was a boy my mother ran a large corporation. She had hundreds of men working for her. She wore Yves Saint Laurent and smoked cigars. The Shah had his faults, but what those

idiots don't realise is, this new lot will be far worse.'
The Ten o'clock news showed mobs chanting death to
the Shah. 'This is all they will show of Iran now - fanatics
chanting in the streets. No one will speak of Ferdowsi,
Rumi and Hafiz. Do you know, darling, the Persians
worship their poets more than they do their prophets.'

Everyone was abandoning the Shah. He was little
more than a refugee, albeit one with a juggernaut of
gold. Even so, no country would take him; Britain and
America turned their backs on their old friend. Pasha
said they should be ashamed of themselves.

'Everyone has betrayed him. Friends will stick
the knife in. And they know where you bleed most.
Yes baby it's cold outside.' He always said this when
the world disappointed him. For days he remained in
the apartment with Rachel. It was as if the world had
betrayed Pasha too. Rachel tried to sweeten his bitterness
with hot tea and tenderness. They lay on the floor. She
held him and loved the way he needed her.

Later, he lined his cards up on the floor again, why, at
forty, had he fallen in love?

'All my life I've been lucky in business. Perhaps at
last I will be lucky in love.' They made love and he barely
moved inside her, yet when he did it was enough to send
shocks of warmth through her. The room was pitch black
and yet she could feel his gaze. The flames in his pupils
burnt into hers and something more powerful than self-
disgust took over. For the first time in her life she felt
beautiful. She could feel herself growing into someone
different beneath his gaze. Heat filled her as he moved
deeper and began to move faster and then he screamed
loudly into the blackness and it was only when she
brushed her hair off her damp brow that she discovered it
wasn't him screaming, but her.

Rachel waited in her tower on the tenth floor. Her
frustration turned to fear, fear that crept under the door
like a draft and formed the words - he has left you; he
has found the strength he said he lacked.

She decided to go out. She walked towards the

front door, pulled the heavy brass hinge towards her and stared through the gap into the expensive carpeted hallway looming silent and eerie.

What if he called? She slammed the door shut. She walked back into the studio with its white walls and sat back down on the pea green sofa. She wondered what Kitty, her sister was doing, whenever Rachel rang, Kitty was busy. Her excuse was she was studying for her exams; more likely hanging out with her mates. Kitty had always been the out-going one. Rachel was more detached. She had her set of friends and yet she always wondered if they were her friends. Things were said behind her back like 'it's alright for her' and 'she's not even that pretty.' Girls didn't get what all the fuss was about. Rachel barely acknowledged there was a fuss, and when she did, she thought it misplaced. She didn't dare think she was pretty; she was trying too hard to make herself liked. Yet the girls, even her set, kept their distance, their wariness intact, their antenna tuned to the slightest sign that she was pleased with herself. She tried too hard to be one of the crowd; she ended up feeling like a fake.

Later that afternoon, a light tapping on the door interrupted the silence. He must've forgotten his key but when she opened the door it wasn't him standing there, but two men, tall and about thirty. Both wore blue suits that had a slight sheen to them and loose ties with the top button of their shirts undone.

'Detective Sergeant Wilkins.' A man with short sandy hair showed Rachel his identification. 'Mind if we have a look around?' They gazed over the furniture taking in her books and a photograph Pasha had the photographer at the club take of her.

'Does the name Marianne Flood mean anything to you?' said the sandy haired cop.

'No.' The detectives were staring. Surely, she thought, they didn't arrest girls for going out with older men. Men more than twice their age. Men old enough to be their father.

The other detective stood beside the sandy haired

one. They avoided looking at one another, and hovered like they were not sure what to do. It hadn't occurred to Rachel that cops might not know what to do. They always seemed so damn sure of themselves on the telly.

'How long have you been living here?'

'Six months. It's my boyfriend's flat.' One of the detectives started walking round the room as if he was taking in every detail. 'This Marianne Flood,' her voice trembled, 'was she a call girl?'

'Why do you ask?

'This apartment block is known for them isn't it? And men phone sometimes asking if they can come over.' Rachel knew the detectives with their quizzical expressions couldn't work out if she was a call girl too.

'My boyfriend doesn't like me answering the phone.'

'Does everything here belong to you?'

'Yes.'

'Where's your boyfriend?' Rachel thought it would look strange if she told them she didn't know so she said he was at work. The phone started to ring. Rachel didn't want to answer it in front of the cops and she knew it wasn't Pasha because he always rang twice and hung up before ringing back. Pasha told everyone to use this code.

'Aren't you going to answer that?'

Rachel went and picked up the phone.

'Hello.'

The line went dead.

'Who was that?'

'I don't know, they hung up.' Rachel didn't tell them that once she answered and a man speaking Farsi swore and shouted down the phone. Pasha thought it might be the glass-eyed chef he sacked who turned out to be a supporter of the Islamic revolution. Persians were switching allegiances and informing on one another all over the shop and Pasha's establishments were known supporters of the previous regime.

Rachel didn't want to tell the cops she had a Persian boyfriend. She clocked the looks and whispers, the prejudice that followed them if they tried a new restaurant or went somewhere Pasha wasn't known. It was why they nearly always went to the same places. The two cops walked towards the door in sudden hurry to leave.

'Thanks for you help.' Rachel didn't want them to leave, but couldn't think of anything to stop them. After, the studio felt empty and instead of plunging back into still life she grabbed her coat and forced herself out.

Downstairs in the lobby she handed her key to the porter standing behind his polished mahogany desk and asked if there were any messages. The porter disappeared into the back office to double-check.

The lobby with its leather armchairs and plants was empty. Rachel remembered the thrill it gave her the first time he brought her here. For a month he hadn't touched or kissed her. And then he told he was taking her away for the weekend, but the club had been busy that Friday so they hadn't gone anywhere and after the club finished he brought her here. As he led the way through the swirling glass door Rachel couldn't help the feeling that what they were doing was strangely illicit. It sent a shivery excitement down her spine. The porter returned. There were no messages.

Matthew Rhodes
Scarecrows

Jack pours himself another Jamesons and coke. His hands shake. Two in the morning and his face is paraded across all the twenty-four hour news channels. Eyes are red and puffy from the Niagara Falls that has been rolling down his cheeks all night. The news keeps repeating itself. They'll interview more people when daylight comes back again and the rest of the world awakes to the news. Then they can go on Facebook and Twitter to officially state their views. Get behind Jack will surely be one of the hashtags used. Then someone will comment on it saying, 'I bet Jack would love that, whaaay.' And this is okay because its banter. British banter. And if you don't like it, then you're just really boring, aren't you?

Time for the newspaper review now and, not surprisingly, the tabloid front pages in particular are dominated by pictures of Norwich City and England international Jack Fulton after he revealed that he is gay on his Twitter account. He becomes only the second British football player to announce his homosexuality.

Jack finally turns the TV off. He looks at his mobile. Thirty-four unread messages. He downs his glass and rubs his eyes. He picks up his mobile again and reads the message sent from his agent.

Jack, you ok? I'm not sure if this has been a good idea. The players will be fine with it. The club will be fine with it. The fans will be fine. But you know who won't be...

Another knot is tied in his stomach as he reads the last line. Jack recalls Faye Burlock's mouth practically foaming when the story broke on the news.

"It's football's last taboo," she declares, witch-like. She interviews former players and managers with a zest for shit-stirring.
"He's brave."
"He's done the right thing."
"This is a landmark moment."
"Good on him."
"Football's attitudes have changed over time..."
Etc. etc. say the players and managers interviewed.
"But what kind of reaction is he going to get from supporters?"
"Won't he be worried by what supporters will say?"
"Won't he be forced to retire?"
"Does he realise what he's done?"
"Does he know how it ended for Justin Fashanu?"

This is all Faye Burlock can come up with. Controversy dribbling out of her media-trained garbage hole that blows hot gossip air into our atmosphere every weekday afternoon.

Jack's agent sends him another text.

Sleep on it. Take tomorrow off training. Whatever you do, DO NOT read any comments sections on any website. DO NOT read the lowest rated comments. They're the lowest rated for a reason.

Five days later. Saturday, Jack's first game since coming out. Norwich are playing away at Aston Villa.
'WHAT KIND OF RECEPTION WILL HE GET?' bleats every tabloid as they jump on the hype train.
'HOW BADLY WILL HE BE AFFECTED' the broadsheets join in unconvincingly. 'WILL HE BE ABLE TO CONTINUE HIS GOOD FORM FOR CLUB AND COUNTRY', the Prime Minister is asked.

It's not just the Prime Minister getting asked this.

Everyone is asking this on TV. Let's hear what Giles Brandreth has to say about it on The One Show, shall we?

If that isn't enough, let's hear what Tim Lovejoy has to say about the matter whilst he looks into his fame mirror.

Let's hear what all the stand-up comedians have got to say about Jack coming out? Oh look, Frankie Boyle has come out with something ridiculously offensive. Hahaha. It's funny because he's edgy. And if you don't like it, then that's just your fault and you probably like Michael McIntyre and you should feel bad about yourself for liking light-hearted observational humour.

Sky are the worst though. They have a special Player Cam fixed just on Jack Fulton for the Villa vs Norwich match. You can follow his every move. Every gay move.

The match was not even scheduled for live TV coverage. Now suddenly it is. Sellout crowd too.

The Sky Sports presenter says to us plebs that the important thing to focus on is the match and not individual players. He has said this for about the seventh time now and each time we see images of Jack doing a modelling shoot whilst he says it.

So the players come onto the pitch and Jack gets a hero's reception. 'There's only one Jack Fulton' shout the Villa and Norwich fans in unison as soon as he steps on Villa Park's turf. Jack applauds both sets of fans as he tries to bottle his emotions. Cameras follow his every move. They ignore the giant sign held up by numerous Norwich fans that reads 'RESPECT FOR JACK'.

Norwich win 2-1. Fulton wins man of the match and attracts praise for his superb assist for the Canaries' second goal. He declines all post-match interviews. He's already said what needs to be said. Better to take the Paul Scholes approach to media now.

Everyone praises Jack's performance after the match. He leaves Villa Park a hero. A real role model.

Someone who has actually made a lasting impact on the sport for good.

So there you have it. He went on to have an excellent career. Sixty-four international caps isn't something to be sniffed at. Ultimately, he broke the last taboo.

The end.
Oh. Ah, yeah. I forgot.
That isn't actually the ending.
We live in England, right?
Here's how it ends.

The newspapers send out their goon squads for the following month to harass Jack. They speak to a former lover of his. Sells his story for five hundred grand (what a good egg). Heavily implies two other Premier League footballers he has slept with. Doesn't name them in person but even your average Sun reader can join up the dots.

Faye Burlock's shit-stir foghorn begins to ring again. How many other footballers has Jack slept with?

How will they be able to cope with all this speculation if they don't want to reveal their sexuality?

Oh no, what has Jack done?

Then comes the death threats. The fallouts. The pictures. Oh yeah, forgot to mention. One of the tabloids manages to secretly film Jack at a club with his fancy man. He's blissfully unaware each kiss, each embrace, each drink and every single good time is being photographed for the nation to gawp at. The pictures are all on display for England's attention the morning after.

Jack's form on the pitch deteriorates. The players Jack is

romantically linked with also have a drastic decline in form. Their fans aren't happy and they know who to blame.

Some people speak out about the tabloids. They are shouted down. Not by reason but they are literally just shouted down.

"Well, Jack Fulton's private life is in the media's interest now. He chose to come out on Twitter. I can't think of anything more public than that. Everybody now wants to know about Jack and this is reflected in our extended coverage of him. If he didn't want all this coverage in his private life, then he shouldn't have come out should he," says one of the leaders of the goon squads on Breakfast TV.

He smiles as he says this. A slow smile. How can someone's smile be so unnerving?

Jack is dropped from England's squad for the forthcoming European Championships.

Two days later, Faye Burlock wears her funeral face and emphasises every word she speaks for dramatic effect.

"Our main story this morning is the breaking news that Jack Fulton has been found dead at his house. A suicide note was apparently left in the same room."

Then she ends the first main report of the story with this. "Who is to blame for this young, talented man's tragic death?"
Who is to blame?
On the following Saturday after Jack's death, a strange thing happened.

Mid-December. When all the Saturday 3pm games reach the seventy-first minute, the matches are all being played under late afternoon floodlights.
Then the floodlights fail. At every single stadium in the UK. All the players stand motionless in every single

game being played across the country. Like scarecrows. Just dotted around the pitch in a frozen state. All the crowds stare at them in silence as if in hypnosis. No chants. No criticisms of the manager. Nothing.

Then after about two minutes in this pause mode, the players on each pitch in the UK walk off the pitch in complete silence. They don't even speak to each other. All the fans file out of the stadiums too. Players and fans alike leave the sport behind in darkness without making a sound.

"Who is to blame?" says the Prime Minister.

"Who is to blame?" says the News.

"Who is to blame?" says Nuts magazine.

"Who is to blame?" says The One Show (following a feature on Kris Akabusi walking around his parents house and saying, "Wow, this hasn't changed a bit").

"Who is to blame?" says Tim Lovejoy (whilst looking at the mirror).

"Who is to blame?" says all the tabloid back pages in unison.

Roy Marshall
Above the Brim

A manager who'd arrived fresh-faced in '64
recalled the endless drive from gate to office,
a daunting walk across the floor through air thick
with metal slough and the beat of loud machines.

Workers told of crushing boredom, of toilet trips
timed by foremen, line speeds increased until hands
were a blur. A steward, from the foundry where
engine blocks were forged, spoke of a lopped finger

taken by a cat, and one woman remembered the hat
worn in honour of a visit by the second Henry Ford.
Skilled machinists, paid as unskilled, sat at their benches
and roared, as Ada greeted him, respectful and demure,
'Bollocks' stitched clearly above the brim.

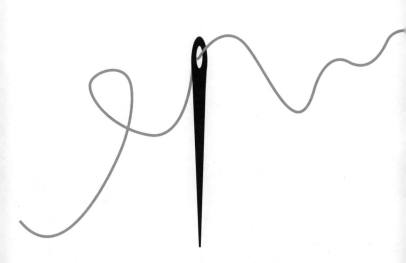

Roy Marshall
Downpour

An arc from a gutter
splatters a baptism
onto the heads of boys in shorts
who shout as they dance
through this glassy fluke
as if they've broken free
from two-tone frames
shot in another century.
        Pan from white wings
that fledge their black-shod feet:
follow the flood, cigarette butts at its lip,
until it's swallowed by a mouth
with iron teeth, a city born river
gone in search of sea.

Sue Bodnar
Extracts from Imogen Clancy

1 – Look What the Cat Dragged In

Imogen Clancy knelt down in front of her dog, sucked her top lip, and concentrated as hard as she could. Then she repeated the question, slowly.

'Are...you...someone...else?'

Mike looked at her for a moment before yawning a load of foul doggy breath into her face.

'Ugh!' Imogen recoiled, leaning back on her heels as Mike stretched out across the sofa. Once she'd recovered, she moved back, closer this time, until her nose was only a few centimetres from Mike's. Imogen flicked back her long fringe, and stared into his big, furry face. He looked slightly awkward at first, trying to avert his huge eyes, but once he'd noticed the big star-shaped button on her cardigan, he became transfixed. The temptation was too much and he lunged towards the button, chewing at it gleefully.

Imogen sighed with disappointment.

I don't know why you're bothering, said the voice in Imogen's head, which was not her own. She looked around her, scanning the room for signs of life.

The creature's a complete imbecile! You may as well be talking to a doughnut for all the good it'll do you.

Then she noticed the grey bushy tail poking out from beneath the curtain, slowly swishing from side to side. Imogen pulled back the curtain, and sure enough, there was Poopsydoodles sitting on the windowsill, surveying the street outside.

I remember when all this was fields, you know, when I was a lad.

'But you're a girl cat,' said Imogen, rolling her eyes. 'We've just had you neutered so you won't have kittens. You can't have been a "lad".'

Poopsydoodles looked Imogen up and down with the utmost disgust, then licked her paw and began to clean around the back of her ears.

You youngsters these days. Haven't got the brains you were born with. When I was your age I was already working in father's shop, and helping mother with the household duties, as well as running errands for...

'Oi! Hang on. You're a complete fat liar! What do you mean, 'when you were my age'? You are five months old. I am ten years old! If you were my age, you'd probably be dead.'

You cheeky scamp! You're not too big for a good hiding you know!

Imogen grabbed Poopsydoodles and held her up beneath her shoulders so her front paws stuck out like a sleepwalker. The cat glared her hardest glare, prompting Imogen to laugh.

'Oh, Poopsydoodles, you're so cute when you're trying to be fierce.'

The name is Hastings! Clarence Hastings. You won't get away with this, young lady. As soon as this mix up has...

But Imogen had picked up a toy mouse filled with catnip and was waving it just out of Poopsydoodle's reach.

Don't you think you can get around me by.... ok, give me the mouse and we'll say no more about it.

Imogen dangled it a bit further away.

Give me the mouse! Give me the mouse. Give it, give it, give it, give it, give it!

Imogen threw the mouse as far as she could, out of the lounge, down the hall and into the kitchen. With a huge push, Poopsydoodles leapt out of her arms and pelted off after it. Imogen watched as her cat skidded around the kitchen door, spotted the mouse, and poised to attack. Then, with a loud 'Say your prayers, vermin!' she pounced out of view, leaving Imogen with nothing but a highly satisfied chomping sound to reveal the mouse's fate.

Imogen sat back down in front of the sofa. She gazed at Mike who was curled up asleep, completely still except for the odd flick of his ear. This had been a very odd day for Imogen Clancy, which was saying something, as Imogen's days generally scored pretty highly on the odd-ometer. Today's oddness, though, was completely off the scale. Until today, Poopsydoodles had been a normal, everyday sort of cat. Technically still a kitten, even though she was fully grown, she'd chased bits of string, chewed at the furniture, and ran up the curtains for no apparent reason. Normal.

But then she went to the vet's for her operation, and ever since they'd brought Poopydoodles home a few hours ago, Imogen could hear a voice in her head. The voice was that of a very posh, and somewhat grumpy old man, who said that he was trapped inside Poopsydoodle's body.

Imogen didn't know what to think, which was why she'd tried to talk to Mike to see if he had something similar going on. It seemed he didn't. Mike began to snore in little snuffly growls and Imogen watched with amusement as his tail twitched back and forth as he dreamt of chasing rabbits. Mike had very short, wiry, black fur all over his body, apart from the end of his tail. Here it was considerably longer, like a pom-pom, and whenever he stuck his tail up in the air, it looked like a microphone. Which was why they'd called him Mike. Imogen decided she needed to question Poopsydoodles some more.

Having strange voices in her head wasn't new to her, but they'd never been so clear and distinct before. And they'd certainly never been so rude or foul-tempered. She gave Mike a little stroke between the ears, then got up and headed for the kitchen. Poopsydoodles was beneath the dining table, purring loudly, and still chewing on the mouse which was clasped between her front paws. When Imogen crouched down to look at her, she started to growl.

'Poopsykins! Don't be silly. I'm not going to take your mouse off you.'

Of course you're not, child. And pigs fly! Do you think I was born yesterday?

'Erm, I don't know. It's possible I suppose.'

Imogen crawled right under the table towards the cat,

who promptly curled herself protectively around her toy. The modern youth... you'd rob your own grandmother at the drop of a hat on a sawdust plank, for half a crown and thruppence.

'What?! Why would anyone want to steal one half of a crown? Why not just take the whole thing? And what's 'thruppence'? I totally have no idea what you're babbling on about!' Imogen giggled, as she reached out to tickle Poopsydoodle's neck.

'That's exactly what I was thinking,' said another voice, definitely not inside Imogen's head. She looked up to see a large pair of feet in front of her, wearing dark green socks with the word 'Thursday' knitted into them. Her heart sank as she realized Dad had overheard her. This could only mean one thing.

*

2 – Crime and Purr-nishment

Imogen Clancy pressed the 'illuminate' button on her digital watch for the twenty-second time. It wasn't necessary, as there was still enough light for her to see that it had been seventeen long minutes since Dad had told her to sit quietly until Mum got home. He'd put Poopsydoodles outside, and then left Imogen sitting by the table, 'to think about what she'd done'.

She pressed the 'illuminate' button again, wishing Mum would hurry up so she could get 'The Little Chat' over with. Then she wished that she had an illuminate button on the side of her face which would light up her features from beneath her skin. She imagined the look on her parents' faces and began to giggle. She promised herself to remember that look while they were talking to her.

Imogen had grown to hate 'The Little Chat', which was a total failure of a name on two counts: first, it was never little. They always went on for ages and ages and ages, until Imogen thought she would actually just go completely rigid and die of boredom. Second, it wasn't a chat. Mum and Dad would just talk at her, and then ask her some questions without ever listening to the answer.

'Click!' Mum's key turned in the door and Mike instantly bounded out to greet her.

'Here we go,' thought Imogen, wishing she could just disappear.

A few minutes later, Mum and Dad were sitting opposite her looking very concerned.

'We've been through this a hundred times, sweetheart! You need to end this nonsense about imaginary friends!' said Mum.

'But...' said Imogen.

'Remember Doctor Sprudelhoff's orders; stop pretending to hear voices!' said Dad.

'But...'

'And no more making up fantasies about people having 'ghost' faces!' said Mum.

'But...'

'It's very disappointing,' said Dad.

'We got you that cat to help you,' said Mum.

'And this is how you repay us?!' said Dad.

Imogen started to count all the little bits of boiled egg stuck in Dad's beard. She wondered if there was an entry in the Guinness Book of Records for 'Most Egg Contained in One Beard'. And if the judges would have to count all the bits, or get them all out and weigh them. And would the record-holder have a special title like King of the Eggy Beards? Or maybe just King Eggbeard, which sounded a bit like a Viking, whose tribe was...

'Imogen! Are you listening?!' shouted Mum.

'That's agreed then,' said Dad. 'No pocket money for six weeks. See if that snaps you out of it.'

At that point, as she usually does, Mum started to get upset. Dad put his arm around her and led her out of the room. As they were closing the door, Imogen heard Mum say quietly, 'Sometimes I think she does it to punish me, to make me feel guilty, because she knows...' Then the door clicked shut.

Imogen Clancy sat in silence. A big, hollow, outer space sort of silence.

She sucked her top lip.

Then a muffled little voice broke through into her mind. She tried to block it by thinking about the card tricks she liked to do, but it just wouldn't go away. She couldn't ignore it any longer and focused in...

Hell's teeth, girl! Open the blimming door will you, before my joints seize up completely!

Imogen looked up to see Poopsydoodles peering through the kitchen window, nose pressed to the glass, with her front paws cupping her eyes, like she was holding binoculars.

These cold temperatures play havoc with my rheumatism, you know. Now come along!

Imogen got off the chair and placed it carefully back under the table.

She walked out of the kitchen, up the stairs, and into her bedroom, quietly closing the door behind her. Then she did what she always did in these situations: she picked up a deck of playing cards and sat down at her special card table that Nan had given to her. Imogen began to shuffle the pack. Once they were properly mixed, she laid them out on the green felt of the table top for a game of Solitaire.

Turning the cards, and slowly placing them in correctly ordered piles was calming for Imogen, and as soon as she'd finished one game, she immediately started another. Numbers, red, patterns, black, hearts, clubs, jacks, queens. She was about to lay her kings down for the fourth time when she heard scratching at the door.

'Go away!' she snapped.

The scratching continued. Imogen marched to the door and pulled the handle.

'Clear off Poops! I'm not allowed...'

And in walked Mike, his huge tongue lolling out of the side of his mouth...with Poopsydoodles riding on his back.

Well, it's not a patch on the Bentley. Acceleration's erratic and the exhaust is a bit loud and whiffy, but I suppose one has to make do when times are hard. It's what we did in the war.

Imogen's mouth hung open in disbelief as Poopsydoodles jumped down to the floor and walked

nonchalantly towards the radiator. Mike sat down, alert
and panting, hoping for a biscuit.

Give the poor simpleton a reward, would you child.
And while you're at it, I'd like a small meal preparing.
Just some spam and a little chutney will do. Oh, and a
drop of dry sherry, to warm the cockles.

Vicky Morris
Beside the Seaside

If you're gonna lose your screws and slide right up to the other end of the seesaw, it's only right to get as high as Brighton will take you.

Cashless and running off clues as to how I could restore hydration to my fizzing, wizened brain, I protected myself from the train guard by wearing my best suit and flashing him a ticket I found on the floor. I'd scribbled out Sheffield, and written 'Beside-the-Seaside' to get me as far as London. I hopped carriages and screwed myself up into a ball in a compartment packed with bikes, my mead inside my holdall. It was empty but for my shorts and T-shirt lived-in skin and that bucket and spade I found when I had crawled into next door's sand pit to sleep. Here I memorised the speech I would deliver on the beach to the sea near the big wheel.

I'd only visited Brighton once, the week before, whilst cast adrift on the sofa having lost the oars that would allow me to flow out of the front door without the need for flippers to keep me safe. I neglected to pick up my prescription because I needed only salt to cleanse my neurons. I had been ordered to go by my favourite TV presenter. I forget his name, but he looks like me and was wearing the same starched snake-skin armour that had stopped me from breathing many times before. I saw the burnt-out carcass of the West Pier float by behind him in pixels and knew right then that this was my spiritual home.

In the station toilets, I shed my uncivil-servant pay-scales-n-tie to become the beatnik butterfly that had been flapping faster and faster against the light bulb in my head. I read the biroed ads for fuck buddies and

soliloquies on all of the toilet doors, and whispered my
own into a bottle marked 'Best before the cork goes
POP!' Too late, I had thrown away the lid.

If there's one thing I've learnt, I said to the old dear
on the choo-choo, never take your depression to the
promised land of Mecca Bingo. Lithium and candy floss
don't mix. She touched my arm with Halloween fingers
and I thought about how I would soon have the breeze of
life on my wings.

There should have been a welcome sign as I left the
station "The end of a steep ride up!", but the beeswax-
dipped woman in the kiosk outside didn't seem to agree.
A shame because I told her she burns longer like me and
should take advantage of needing very little sleep.

Down on the beach I soaked my feet and found my first
disciple in the form of Derelict Derrick from Denby, who
tried to convince me he wasn't mental despite the legacy
of his town. In the end, he couldn't help but boast about
being one of the last to leave the fortress there, claimed
he and it became derelict together. I said whatever,
it wasn't a problem. God loves all of my children. We
quickly developed a telepathy and fell out over who was
following who. I agreed it was him in the end when it
became apparent he knew road names, the best bins and
the softest grass to sleep on.

Under the stars I thought about my so-called achievements,
the office with the walls that used to move towards me
a few inches every day. It was good we made it outside
I told him. Time scrambled into the corners of movie
montage clips and back in Sheffield I played out in an
endless stream of manic episodes on my TV.

Derrick and I, and a girl called Pob (and her imaginary
dog), spent that summer riding the big dipper together.
We ignored the embers of the skeletal West Pier lurking
on the horizon and focused only on the pleasures of the

Palace lights. We lived on scraps foraged from Waitrose
and took daily baptisms in an ocean of healing salt.

Separately we knew the feeling of being clamped down,
of cold bars pressing our arms back, of being hemmed in,
the jolt of old wood pushing out along rickety, dangerous
tracks, the ride we couldn't control taking us all the way
to the top and then - crash. We knew about spiralling
out of sync on the tight corkscrew bends' getting stuck
upside-down at the end with no maintenance man
willing to climb up and push us into another day.

But that summer, we rode the Palace Pier's big dipper
together. We rode it like we invented the ride. And we let
it carry us away.

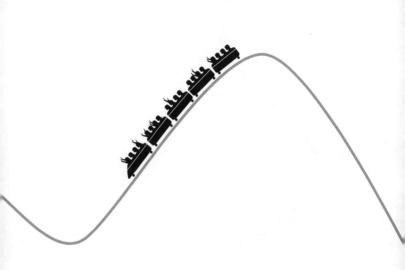

Danuta Reah
Chapter 1: The Equations of Death

1st September 1942

The Litzmannstadt Ghetto, Lodz, Poland

The room stank. It smelt of fear, of disease, of poor sanitation. People huddled on the floor. Dirty rags that had once been curtains and blankets hung here and there in an attempt at privacy. In the darkness, children whimpered with hunger.

Levi Kahne crouched on the floor beside the thin mattress where his wife and sons lay. There had been no ration today. He had been given a cup of thin soup at the workshop, and the boy, Orin, had managed, somehow, to get a piece of bread. Sarah had tried to feed the baby, but though he sucked ravenously, they both knew her milk was failing. Nature had made its decision. Sarah's body was too depleted for her to feed her child. Josek, just six months old, was too fragile to live.

The children had fallen asleep at last. Even then, Josek whimpered and stirred. Sleep was not enough to quell the hunger now. Only death would do that. And death was coming. Levi was sure of that.

He shifted as his bones pressed against the hard wall. He needed to sleep. Sleep would be an escape. Sleep would take him away for a few hours, but he couldn't afford it now. He had sworn to protect his family, and, desperate though things were, worse things were on their way. Early that morning, the soldiers had come into the ghetto. Cordons of guards surrounded the hospital, and the sick were dragged out, loaded into trucks and driven away. The Nazis had no use for the weak and the unproductive. The writing was on the wall and Levi could read what it said.

He had to find a way out. He had been a mathematician in the other life, the life he and Sarah had lived before the world went crazy. Logic was his trade, but now, when he needed logic like he had never needed it before, hunger left him almost incapable of rational thought. He looked at the children lying with their mother on the bed. He saw that Orin was awake, his dark eyes fixed on his father. Josek still slept. If he woke, he would cry until he lost the energy to do even that. Levi wished with all his heart that his youngest son had never been conceived. This was not a world to bring a child into.

Soon, tomorrow, maybe the next day, they would come for the children. He knew that as surely as he knew the moon would rise. They would take both boys, drag them from their mother's arms and throw them into the trucks. The children, alone and terrified, would be taken away like the sick and injured had been. And then? No one knew, but there were rumours. All Levi knew for sure was that no one who had been deported from the ghetto had ever been heard from again.

He had to save his children. He had to make a decision. He had to do the best he could for his family. And now the power of logic returned and showed him how meagre his best could be. The facts formed themselves into an equation, and the equation balanced on dreadful scales. On one side, Orin lived. On the other, Josek died. It was as simple as that. Babies could not survive here.

But Orin? Orin might - just - live. He was a tough child with a small, wiry body and a single-minded determination. Already, he was developing the survival skills the ghetto demanded. If he was given a chance, he might just make it.

Levi knew of a place where he could hide one child, a child who knew enough to be still and silent. The equation balanced. The answer was inevitable. When they came for the children – and they would come, he knew that – then he, Levi, would take Josek gently in his arms and, before the child could have any awareness, he would dash his son's brains out against the stone mantel. The

Germans would not have him.

Could he make himself do that?

Logic. The equation.

He reached into his pocket. The twist of paper was still safe. Sugar, just a small amount. He'd stolen it from the supplies stored in the office of Chaim Rumkowski, the Jewish leader of the ghetto. If Rumkowski found out he had taken it, then Levi would hang. If you were one of the well-born, if you were a friend of Rumkowski, then you got more, but Levi counted for nothing in Rumkowski's world.

He offered up a prayer even though he was no longer a believer. No just God could allow this suffering to happen, not to the innocent, not to the helpless. If there was a God in this world, then it was men like Rumkowski, men like the Germans, who were made in His image, and Levi would not bend the knee to such a God.

He filled a cup with water, a small amount, and carefully dissolved the sugar. He detached the baby from Sarah's arms, and as the small mouth opened in protest, he spooned in the first of the syrup. In moments, the child had finished it all. Levi tensed, in case Josek would cry in protest that there was no more, but the exhaustion of hunger and its brief assuagement made the child's eyelids droop, and carried him back to the safe world of sleep. Levi looked down at his son's face, at the closed lids, almost translucent in their perfection. The baby's face was pinched, and he felt light in his father's arms. He wasn't growing like a child should. Levi's eyes stung and he felt a pain in his stomach that was more than hunger. 'Josek,' he whispered. Carefully, quietly, he got to his feet, his infant son cradled inside his coat. It was after curfew, but he had to take his chances.

He picked his way across the bodies lying on the floor. The people crammed in here had tried to partition the room with blankets, but with ten people in this tiny space, they had to manage the best they could.

'You OK, Levi?' That was Adam, another man who walked the line of keeping his family alive every day of the week. Levi almost told him about the equation, but instead huddled the bulk of the infant further inside his coat and gestured to his stomach. Adam nodded. Sickness and diarrhoea were endemic in the ghetto, a killer that took so many of the young and the weak.

Levi crept down the narrow stairway, wondering as he always did how they would escape if the houses burned. Sometimes he dreamed of the flames, flames that devoured every one of them, every man, every woman and every child. Then he was out on the midnight street. He headed towards Lutomierska, where the bridge crossed the main road, to the Catholic church of St Mary. He moved quickly, keeping to the shadows. Within half an hour, he was back. His arms were empty. He moved across the room to the place where his family lay. Tomorrow, he would have to tell Sarah.

Tomorrow.

Orin's gaze met his in the darkness. Levi turned his face away and wept.

*

Four days later, the soldiers returned to the ghetto and the children were taken.

Bruce Barnes
When I-

give up the ghost,
it will be to a wraith whose need
is more substantial than mine.
When I kick the bucket,
it will ring with a steely cry
at so much spilt milk.
When I buy the farm
the estate agent will sing
the praises of its topsoil.
When I pop my clogs,
the coffin maker will provide
a steadier percussion.
When I go the way of all flesh
the motorway will be gridlocked
by a cortege of butchers' vans.

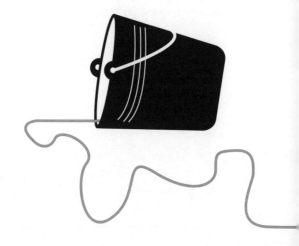

Bruce Barnes
Repair

In a blast of warmth, I hand over a watch
with fingers that keep on massaging the face
between 5 and 10 past 7, its manipulative tips
drawing across a frozen hour. She cradles it.
I say: "I think it's the battery"-

I think it was that hour when the Park reduced to frost;
boughs stood their ground against a cold that pinched the body
to its skin. I became less than when I set out.

She finger-tips a silvered pea and slips into
the cramped space where a man is absorbed with fixing
an upper to a sole. Her hand snakes out for pliers.
The watch lid won't close; there is an opposing force,
as if moment were springy, like shoving jack in a box.

Rebecca McCormick
It Shook Right Through My Spine

I'm five, seven, maybe nine. Summer holidays are a rare
and precious thing, a time when both my parents are off
work and focussed solely on me. While my friends are
going on aeroplanes to places called Estartit and Malta,
we are hitching up the caravan to the car and taking a
slow, laborious trundle down Europe. When we arrive we
set up camp and commence battle with the locals using
my dad's schoolboy French and my mother's dogged
insistence that they speak "lentement, lentement."
France is long, wide highways with fields either side, rest
stops with strange loos, glaces and saucisse-frites, big
waves, sunshine, sunflower fields and Simon & Garfunkel,
Bridge Over Troubled Water. It's been taped off the vinyl
by my dad and it stops halfway through Cecilia.

"I am just a poor boy," my dad sings when The Boxer
plays, and always, always puts the 'tssch' of the cymbal
in after the 'Lai la lai'. After his death I always put the
'tssch' in too, as a tribute.

*

I'm eight years old and we've been to the Olympics in
Barcelona, although we're staying in the very south of
France in the caravan again. I get stung by a jellyfish
trying to catch it. I eat prawns for the first time.
I swing on the green swings in the campsite's playground
one night, and come across two teenagers, each in a
plaid shirt and scruffy jeans, grunge style. It's almost
fully dark, and each camp area is lit up, with adults
gathered on folding chairs, cradling plastic cups of wine.
At the swings it's really dark, just the glint of green metal
coming through. The boys are singing a song, sweetly

harmonising with each other.

I am fourteen before I can put a name to the song I heard. A friend plays it on one of those cold, dark nights filled with cigarette smoke that seem to go on forever when you're fourteen. The song is Knocking On Heaven's Door by Guns 'n' Roses.

I'm older than I ought to be before I realise that theirs is a cover version. Bob Dylan has to grow on me but I love him in my 20s. My friend Laura and I drive to Whitby with Biography on our iPods one cold spring day when we are twenty-two, singing along and laughing at Laura's terrible impression of Bob.

*

I'm thirteen. It's February 1997 and Blur are about to release a new album. This is great because me and couple of my friends already love their old ones. We have tickets to see them at Leeds Town & Country Club (now slickly rebranded as an O2 Academy). I have wide black trousers and a lacy white top and I think I look the absolute shit. We stand really near the front, on Graham's side. They're touring the new album though, and given that this is the time before pirated leaks and illegal downloading, we don't have a clue about the new songs.

Years later, everyone will tell me that they prefer Blur's later stuff like Think Tank. A wanky few will insist that they "really loved Modern Life Is Rubbish, actually," despite the fact that they were about six when it came out. The Great Escape remains my Blur album, though, something that I can play for comfort and distraction years later.

In 2009 I see Graham Coxon play with Pete Doherty, and I am more excited about him than I am about Peter. It's Graham Coxon, after all.

"Oh," my mum says. "The one with glasses from Blur." She has been trained well.

*

I'm twenty-one and getting married. After a bad experience at our engagement party, we hand pick two hundred songs, make a bunch of CDs and present them to the DJ.

He plays Nellie the Elephant, which was a single before most of us were even born. Everyone, young and old, dances, making a mosh pit on the dancefloor of the nice hotel. I, the bride!, get slammed off the floor and sit with my new grandparents-in-law, watching everyone else pogo madly.

Towards the end of the night the DJ, an old punk himself, declares that he can't believe the reaction the song got, so he's going to play it again. This time, he joins in with the dancing.

Afterwards, it's the music that everyone talks about. It's the music that made our wedding stand out.

*

I'm twenty-four and I'm getting my first tattoo. The very cute tattooist knows the lyric that she's inking on to my inner forearm and we discuss the band and the gigs we've been to. When I've got the music, I've got a place to go. Rancid are one of my favourite punk bands, one of the very few bands that both Lee and I like.

Barely six weeks later my dad jumps off a bridge suffering from psychosis and drowns, leaving us in shock and heartache. He didn't like tattoos, but two weeks before his death he told me he liked mine. I cherish this moment like so many others.

In the months following his death, there is so much music that I can't listen to. Music he liked, music I love but which he mocked, anything by Joy Division. I retreat into shitty pop punk, because it's easy to listen to and has no associations with my dad. One day on the way home from work I'm listening to a band I love sing about how "things have changed for me, but that's okay". I break down crying on the side of the motorway because things have definitely changed, but it's not oh-fucking-kay.

*

I'm twenty-eight and my mum and I go to see Bruce Springsteen in Manchester. It's the only stadium gig I've ever been to (preferring to usually stick to venues where I can see the whites of the drummer's eyes) and we're really, really high up. My mum grabs on to the moustachioed fella in a cowboy hat next to her when she gets vertigo. Springsteen is amazing, he plays for hours without so much as a breather.

Bruce songs are part of my psyche. They run through me like words through a stick of seaside rock. You don't have to be from mid 50s America to understand them; I'm from Yorkshire, from where Thatcher closed the pits and stole the milk, but I feel them, I deeply feel them.

When he plays The River, a song about first love and doing what's right and life not turning out like you thought it would, there are tears in my eyes and I raise my head to the dreary Manchester sky and say a silent thankful prayer to my dad.

*

I'm twenty-five and two friends and I have come to see The Academy Is. They're supporting someone we don't want to see, so by 8pm we're outside the venue in the dusk, feeling the heat of the day dissipate. Manchester is never quiet and tonight is no different. Buses pass the venue, students tumble out of bars and bright takeaways belch out hot grease.

The drummer invites us along for a drink with the band. We walk with him and a roadie to a narrow bar between an Oxfam and a flower shop. It has comfortable red leather banquettes around low tables. The drummer goes to the bar. We sit down. The singer comes to chat with us. One of the guitarists, Mike, comes over after William. He has a reputation for being quiet around fans. We, however, can't shut him up. He talks about their show, their music, and their missing bass player (absent tonight due to a severed tendon in his finger). He jokes about the perils of irons in hotel rooms. He talks about the band he almost joined but about how he was still in school when they went on tour. This band is much more famous and makes serious money; I do wonder if he regrets it. He swears a lot, peppering his speech with "Fuck yeah!" and "Fuckin' A!"

We ask him what kind of music he likes. Some of it is expected (bloody Foo Fighters), some is not. He likes female singers like Regina Spektor and Metric, and he likes Ryan Adams. We like Ryan Adams too. I ask if he's ever met Ryan.

Mike shakes his head. "I fuckin' wish," he says, as only a true fan can.

William comes back and offers my friend a sip of his drink when she isn't sure what to order. We chat to him and I tell him that his music has helped me get through the year since my dad died. He asks how he died and I'm honest; I don't see the point in covering it up. He hugs me and says that he's been there, that he sympathises, and that he's sweetly honoured that his music has helped me.

Being able to tell him is an important thing for me. I never understand those bands who dourly proclaim to the NME that 'they're not in it for the fame, man'. What would be the point, then? You make music to try to reach out to people, to share something, to try to forge meaning across the void. Otherwise, what would be the point?

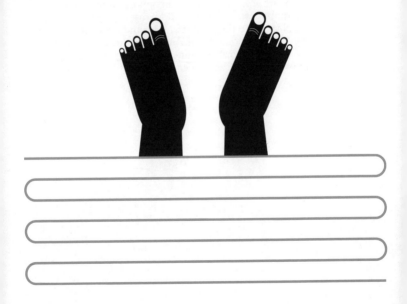

Sean O'Brien
Natalie, Natalie

Too much white sky, and a raw stubbled field
On the edge of some serious north.
Hit the sod with a spade and it rings.
There is snow in the wind, the winter
Barely ended when it starts.

Well, something led to this, a stocking draped
Over the lamp in the motel room,
The all-night intermittent monologue
Behind the wall, the sleepless insight:
Because formerly Natalie wouldn't –

A police car goes in cold pursuit
Where there appeared to be no road
But only distance. The enormous emptiness
Has waited here forever for this day
In order to ignore it and endure -

But latterly Natalie would. From Eden, Idaho
Via Angel Gate, Montana,
To Lake Disquiet, North Dakota,
And lastly Potter's Field, a mossy
Enclave of the dead the size of Europe.

There the wolves wait patiently
Among the stones for Satanists to come
With drills to disinter some lunch.
Natalie, Natalie, weaving so prettily
Over the bedroom floor again.

There's an officer down
Where the road turns back at the last motel.
The grave is icy and the feet stick out.
Because formerly Natalie wouldn't, but now?
Well she's finally had it with men.

Sean O'Brien
Dialogue in the Multi-Function Room
For Joachim Sartorius

When they announced we'd wrestle with the truth
It seems they meant it literally,
So that while we are in China, it is also
Batley Corn Exchange at 4pm
One winter Saturday in 1964, which means
This is eternity. Kent Walton commentates.
One in, one out: as Kendo Nagasaki leaves,
So Billy Two Rivers flies in from the ropes.
When words give place to image, sense
To its performance, afternoon
To thirsty dusk, and Johnny Kwango
High fives evil Mick McManus, can it be
That I alone grow weary of a sport
That everybody knows is fixed?
Two falls or a submission to the
Ineluctable forces of history –
A phone call, the need for a piss,
The summons to drill in the hot white square
Beneath the oompah shouting-music.

What is our subject? That is the question.
Let us turn grotesque disparities
Between distinct symbolic orders to
Rhetorical advantage. Tear his effing head off.
How I hate culture! Yet I do my part –
For did not Ovid is in his exile learn
To pass the time enduring Boston Crabs
And forearm smashes from the Thracian
Mat-men of Constanta, grapple-fans?
Seeing how the world must end
In spectacle, with blood and sand?
Although not yet. I rise and limp
Through sunset while the dialogue
Rages and thuds in the cross-arts shed.
There is an avenue of plane-trees,
Twisted like the Wood of Wrestling Suicides,
Where everybody smokes their phones
And screams inaudibly and then goes back
To put their sweaty trunks on. Und so weiter.

Notes on Contributors

Barnes, Bruce

Bruce Barnes is two thirds of the way through the Sheffield Hallam Writing MA, his first degree course in which English or creativity play a significant part. He began by performing his poetry in a North-East folk club, but he's reformed, and has had poems published in various magazines and anthologies, and has two collections, still appearing on the shelves of Oxfam bookshops: *The Love Life of the Absent-minded*, (Phoenix Press, 1993), *Somewhere Else*, (The Utistugu Press, 2003).

Bestwick, Simon

Simon Bestwick was born in Wolverhampton in the 70s and moved to Manchester when he was 2. He has lived there ever since. He has published two novels and three short story collections.

Bodnar, Sue

Sue is in her third year at Sheffield Hallam University. She usually writes scripts but has recently become more preoccupied with completing her first children's novel. Sue has had poetry in *Magma* magazine, a short play on at the Crucible theatre, and is currently setting up a cross-platform children's writing group at Bank Street Arts.

Emmerson, Steve

Following years in amateur publications, Steve Emmerson was first professionally published in *Just 17* magazine – writing under the pseudonym Emma Stevens! He was commissioned to write *Doctor Who* novels for BBC Worldwide. He's had a script 'in development' with an independent film company, been 'invited' to submit plays for BBC Radio 4, and received interest from major publishers in his picture book texts. A self-employed accountant by day, Steve lives in Barnsley with his wife and son.

Halsey, Alan

Alan Halsey is a British poet. He managed the Poetry Bookshop in Hay-on-Wye from 1979 to 1997. Since 1997, Halsey has lived in Sheffield, working as a specialist bookseller and publishing West House Books.

Lockett, Bob

I wrestle novels mainly but love the challenge of shorter pieces. My wife, Mary, encouraged me to do the English and Film BA in 2009 and the Writing MA was a natural progression. I can't thank her enough for that. The scriptwriting module was invaluable experience for all aspects of my writing and the staff and students I've worked with at Hallam have pushed me and my work further than I ever imagined was possible. Great people, great experience.

Lowes, Virginia

Virginia Lowes works with older people, takes photographs, and enjoys mooching around in woods, cemeteries and older areas of the city, Sheffield, where she now lives.

Norman, Dave

Dave Norman was born a long time ago in the mean streets of rural south Herefordshire's notorious Little Italy district. They didn't even have mobile phones in those days. He has had a lot of jobs over the years but writing is the one that is going to make him rich. He likes dogs. That isn't to say he doesn't like cats but they do make him sneeze.

McCardle, Suzanne

Suzanne's work has appeared in national publications, including *The Rialto* and *Best*, and a number of poetry anthologies. She recently completed the Creative Writing MA at Sheffield Hallam University. Suzanne lives in Leeds and has worked as a life coach, librarian, retail manager, and letter writer for an international medical insurance and rescue company. *Bone Lake* is her second novel.

McCormick, Rebecca

Rebecca McCormick is a self-employed bookkeeper who has always scrawled in a notebook or two. She is a political activist and feminist. She is working on a Young Adult novel about music (her first love) but also writes poetry. Her favourite novelists are Joanne Harris and Carol Goodman, but she also has a sizeable YA collection. She wears a lot of pretty dresses and owns far too much nail polish. This is her first publication.

Marshall, Roy

Roy Marshall lives in Leicestershire where the light in his study is often on until the early hours. His first pamphlet was *Gopagilla* (2012) and a full collection of poems, *The Sun Bathers*, was published by Shoestring Press in 2013. In the same year Roy won the EA Markham award and began an MA at Sheffield Hallam where he is currently enjoying the short story module.

Morris, Vicky

Vicky is an artist, writer and educator. She runs Sheffield and Rotherham Young Writers and works freelance in many creative roles and as part of the development team at Writing Yorkshire. She has edited and designed various publications and anthologies and loves to see words beautifully presented in print. She recently made a documentary about dyslexic writers to change perceptions. Vicky despairs of box-ticking and thrives on creative opportunism. She is particularly proud of her achievements with young writers.

Moss, Linda

Linda Moss is an artist, feltmaker and university lecturer living in the Peak District with a flock of rare-breed sheep and hens. Her first degree, in Russian and Latin, was followed by a PhD in Byzantine cultural history. She is a keen sailor, and has travelled most of the world. She is writing what she hopes will be her debut novel, and has published articles on travel in various magazines.

O'Brien, Sean

Sean O'Brien is a poet, critic, playwright, anthologist, broadcaster, novelist and editor. He grew up in Hull and now lives in Newcastle upon Tyne. He has published seven collections of poetry to date, including *Downriver* (2007) and *November* (2011). His *Collected Poems* was published in 2012.

Reah, Danuta

Danuta Reah, who also writes under the name Carla Banks, was born in South Yorkshire. She comes from an academic family but opted out of formal education at the age of 16. She worked in a variety of jobs from barmaid to laboratory assistant, in a variety of locations, including a brief spell in Kingston, Jamaica. "I didn't plan my working life that way, but it was probably the best apprenticeship a writer could have."

Reval, Mary

I am a lawyer and retired civil servant (diplomat). At the moment, I am taking MA Writing at Hallam.

Rhodes, Matthew

Matthew Rhodes was born in Chesterfield and has lived in Sheffield since late 2011. He mainly writes short fiction mixing dry humour with a surreal twist.

Setterington, Denise

Denise Setterington currently lives in Sheffield where she is working on a project about poetry and dementia. Her work has been published in various magazines and anthologies, including North-East Scotland's *Pushing Out the Boat*. She enjoys reading at spoken word events and working collaboratively with other poets.